GETTING A JOB
AFTER SCHOOL

GETTING A JOB
AFTER SCHOOL

KARLA FITZHUGH

Getting a Job After School

This first edition published by Trotman Publishing, an imprint of Crimson Publishing, Westminster House, Kew Road, Richmond, Surrey TW9 2ND

© Trotman Publishing 2010

Author: Karla Fitzhugh

British Library Cataloguing in Publication Data
A catalogue record for this book is available from the British Library

ISBN: 978-1-84455-266-5

Typeset by RefineCatch Ltd, Bungay, Suffolk
Printed and bound in the UK by Ashford Colour Press, Gosport, Hants

Contents

Contents

About the author

Karla Fitzhugh is an author and journalist who has written many books and articles for young people about education, life choices and life skills, including *The Insider's Guide to Applying to University* and *Which Uni*? (both published by Trotman). Other writing credits include articles for the *Independent*, the *Guardian*, *London Evening Standard* and UCAS magazines. Karla has also provided content for several websites such as www.thesite.org, www.need2know.co.uk and www.apprenticeships.org.uk.

Her website is www.karlafitzhugh.com.

Acknowledgements

· ·

Thank you to everyone who helped with the writing of this book, including Jasmine Birtles, Viviana Rullo, Adrian Wake, Rachel Jobes and all the interviewees who took the time to tell me what their working lives were really like. I'm also grateful to the staff at Trotman Publishing for their advice and hard work, especially Liz Rafii-Tabar and Jessica Spencer.

Special thanks go to Doug Bryson for being generally fabulous, and to Fizz and Disco for not jumping on the keyboard too much while I was typing.

Part 1

Your Options
(or Before you leave)

Chapter 1

Introduction

··

The most recent government statistics* suggest that while 78% of 16 year olds are in full-time education, 13% are in some form of training and nearly 3% are in employment. By the age of 18 years, this changes to about 40% in full-time education, with a further 23% in training and 19% in employment. While there are many books about continuing in education, there's obviously also a great demand for more information about the other options that are available to under-18s.

This book has been created to be a handy resource for any young person who is considering leaving school – either to start work-based training or their first full-time job. It's also a useful reference point for interested teachers, tutors, advisers, parents and carers. The book is divided into three parts:

1. Your Options
2. Directory of Jobs
3. The Toolkit

Part 1: Your Options starts by exploring the most common post-16 choices, and looking at the main pros and cons of each one. It then looks at the best ways to research these choices, to make sure you get the right support and information to make the best decision for yourself. If you then decide that the time is right for you to leave school or college, there are chapters to help you prepare yourself and successfully find the kind of work or training that you're looking for.

Part 2: Directory of Jobs first provides a broad overview of the various employment sectors to give a taster of what's available, and then goes on to cover the different job opportunities within each sector. It details the qualifications, skills and personal qualities needed to do well in these types of work and then looks at relevant information about the labour market, including job prospects. There are also interviews with young people working or training in different sectors, sharing their first-hand experiences. Lastly, contact

*DCSF: Participation in Education, Training and Employment by 16–18 Year Olds in England, released 16 June 2009, author Michael Greer.

details of official bodies that can provide extra advice and support about a particular career are also given.

Part 3: The Toolkit contains lots of practical information to get you through your first weeks of work or training, and beyond. It covers the basics of becoming an employee, from contracts to tax to health and safety. There's also useful advice about leaving home for the first time and living independently. Finally there are tips on how to deal with workplace issues including settling in well, arranging extra training, progressing in your career, and problems such as bullying, harassment, redundancy and unemployment.

Chapter 2
Making the decision to leave school

....

This chapter gives you a brief overview of all your main options if you're still at school. It then goes on to look at some of the pros and cons of each possible choice, to help you think about the general direction that's best for you.

An overview of your options

So, what are your options at the moment? Once you are of school-leaving age (16 years) or older your main choices are to:

1. get a full-time job (with or without some extra part-time study)
2. sign up for apprenticeships or other jobs with training
3. start your own business
4. stay in full-time education (studying academic subjects, or building up your skills to prepare for work).

These are big decisions that can have a massive effect on your life and your general happiness, so don't feel that you have to rush into making your mind up straight away. It's better to take your time, and get as much information as you can together so that you can make the best choices for yourself, based on your research.

All these options have their good sides and their down sides, and different choices suit different people. It can be helpful at this stage to look at the major pros and cons of each choice, to see which of them appeal to you or put you off.

Leaving school: changes in the future

A law has been passed that means that the school-leaving age will change in the future. Young people will have to continue in education or training until the age of 17 from 2013, and until the age of 18 from 2015. If you'd like to find out more about this, search for 'Raising the Participation Age' on the www.dcsf.gov.uk website.

Some of the pros and cons of the various options

As I mentioned earlier, this book is mainly aimed at anyone who is thinking about leaving school and getting a job, or starting an apprenticeship or similar work-based training. However, at this stage let's quickly get an overview of all the options so that you don't rule out any interesting ideas too early on.

Getting a full-time job

On the one hand, getting a full-time job is an attractive option for some people because it means they can start earning money straight away. It also appeals to people who like to learn from direct experience, or who see themselves as the practical sort of person. There is also the possibility that you can 'work your way up through the ranks' of a business, and see your efforts rewarded with time. The more thought you can give right now to the type of work that suits you, the better – try to think about a long-term career if you can, rather than just finding a job to get by for the moment. With the right attitude, and with plenty of commitment and effort, some people who leave school at a relatively young age can eventually become very successful indeed (see some of the famous names on p. 9).

On the other hand, if you have very few qualifications, it is getting harder to find well-paid and interesting jobs that have good prospects for your future. Let's be honest, nobody wants to be stuck in a low-wage, dead-end job for their whole working life. If you have your heart set on leaving school and getting a job as soon as possible you can always decide to get some extra qualifications later, whether that's through weekend or evening courses, or attending courses during the day with the agreement of your employer. There's more information about studying while you're working on page 212.

Important to know

- You are entitled to be paid at least the minimum wage for work you do as soon as you turn 16, unless you're doing an apprenticeship. For more about this, see page 210.
- If you're aged 16–18 and are unemployed, it's often very difficult to get benefits (see p. 211). It's best not to leave school to work if you haven't arranged some sort of employment first.
- There are some jobs that you cannot do unless you have the right degree, diploma or other specific qualification.
- If you're aged under 18 there are some jobs that you are not allowed to do by law, mainly for health and safety reasons.

Working for your family's business

Some young people leave school aged between 16 and 18 so that they can start working for their family business. This can have a lot of plus points but there are also some minus points, so think carefully before you decide. For example:

- O you might get promoted faster, or given special treatment or extra responsibilities

- O if you get on well with your relatives, there can be a great atmosphere in the workplace

- O you could get better wages, a greater share of company profits, or even inherit the business

OR

- O you might get taken for granted, paid very little or end up stuck in a rut

- O your family could have quite set ideas about you, and could push you into doing work that doesn't make good use of your skills and talents

- O sometimes it can be very hard working all day with the people you share a home with, especially if the business isn't going well

- O if you decide to get a different job with a new employer at a later date, a lack of qualifications could be a problem.

It's very useful to talk to friends and family about your research but do make sure that the final decision is yours, rather than something that the people around you might want.

Signing up for apprenticeships or other jobs with training

Signing up for apprenticeships or other jobs which include training can be ideal for some people. You get to gain valuable work experience with an employer, and you also end up with officially recognised qualifications. These qualifications tend to be quite specific to each type of job, so it's important to have a quite firm idea of the sort of career you want before you sign up for anything. That means doing plenty of research, and asking lots of questions before applying for anything. There are different levels of apprenticeship, and some can be at a very high level, such as foundation degree level.

An apprenticeship means working and studying at the same time, and so you'll need plenty of energy and commitment. At the beginning of an apprenticeship, the wages can be relatively low. Sometimes it's hard to juggle the employment and the learning. However, apprenticeships can lead on to much better paid jobs in the future, and might also lead you into higher education later, if that's something you might eventually be interested in. There's a lot more about jobs that include training in Chapter 5 of this book (pp. 33–37).

Important to know
- ○ When you sign up for an apprenticeship, you are signing an employment contract.
- ○ You need to behave in a professional way when you are at work, just like the other employees.
- ○ Most apprenticeships last for one to four years, depending on the level and the type of work.

Starting your own business

Starting your own business isn't something that's done very often by young people who have just left school. But it might still be something that you're interested in trying. If you can set up and run a successful business, there is the chance that you could make large amounts of money. You could also gain a lot of personal satisfaction from being your own boss. However, it's also important to know that many new businesses fail in their first year of trading. Also, you need to be aware that self-employed people usually have to work very hard and very long hours to succeed.

For a business to be successful you need to have a good business plan, a sound knowledge of your market, enterprise skills, advice from professionals in the field, and plenty of ambition, commitment and energy. Many people who decide to start their own businesses first begin by taking a full-time job with an employer in the area of work that they're most interested in. This allows them to find out all kinds of things about how that industry works. In this way they build up their knowledge and experience before taking the plunge and setting up on their own.

If you have a really good idea for a business, and you are prepared to work hard, seek specialist advice and take a chance on yourself then you might like to find out some more about self-employment at this stage. Talk to a school careers adviser or a Connexions adviser (see page 9) or contact some of the organisations listed below.

Starting your own business: contacts
- ○ www.startups.co.uk has an interesting Young Entrepreneurs section.
- ○ http://www.adviceguide.org.uk/index/your_money/employment/self-employment_checklist.htm is a great place to start your research.
- ○ www.shell-livewire.org combines an online support service and awards programme.
- ○ www.princes-trust.org.uk can help you explore and test your business idea.

Staying in full-time education

Staying in full-time education can mean studying academic subjects (and perhaps going on to university or college to study a degree or other qualification). It can also mean building up your basic skills and doing vocational programmes to prepare for work. Generally speaking, the more qualifications you have, the better your chances of finding a well-paid job.

Some people just don't like being at school, and can't wait to leave – and that's okay. Remember, it's completely up to you what you do and don't like. However, it's important to think carefully about whether you truly want to get a job right now or whether you dislike learning in a formal way, or even just dislike the particular school that you're in. For example, you might be happy to continue learning if you were to study different subjects, perhaps more practical or vocational topics rather than purely academic. Or perhaps you might like a change of scenery or staff, and would be happier at a different sixth form, community college or other learning provider.

To find out more about education options in your area and beyond, you can look at your local education possibilities via www.direct.gov.uk/14-19prospectus, speak to a Connexions adviser on 0808 001 3219 (calls are free from a landline), or have a chat with the learning support staff at your school or college.

Important to know
- If you have your heart set on finding a job or apprenticeship but can't get anything suitable, staying in education can at least give you some more qualifications and time to find the right work for you.
- All 16 and 17 year olds who were eligible to leave school in September 2010 are currently guaranteed a place in education or training.
- If you decide to continue learning, you might be entitled to claim the Education Maintenance Allowance (EMA). For more information, visit http://ema.direct.gov.uk.

Other options
Other options include taking a gap year. Most people who do this take a year out to travel, do voluntary work, or get some work experience. A well-planned gap year can look good on a CV, but often it can be expensive. To find out more, try www.gapyear.com.

Successful people who left school at a young age

Billy Connolly, comedian
Sir Alan Sugar, entrepreneur
Jacqueline Wilson, author
Simon Cowell, talent judge and manager
Delia Smith, television cook
Sir Philip Green, entrepreneur
David Beckham, footballer
Sir Michael Caine, actor
Jamie Oliver, chef
Sir Alex Ferguson, football manager

Ozzy Osbourne, musician
Chris Evans, DJ
Julie Burchill, journalist
Sir Richard Branson, entrepreneur
Martin Clunes, actor
John Major, former prime minister
Joss Stone, singer
Guy Ritchie, director
Katie Price (aka Jordan), model and
   businesswoman

Next steps

This chapter should have already given you a few ideas about whether you're ready to leave school or college. Now is a good time to think about key skills you have gained, coursework you've already had marked, and how well you are likely to do in your exams. Consider how this might affect your options, whether it increases them or narrows them down.

Whether you decide to leave education now or in the future, sooner or later most of us will end up in the world of work. So it's never too soon to start thinking about careers. Perhaps you already have a few ideas about the work you'd like to do, but don't worry if you're not sure yet because you still have time to do some research and make up your mind. Remember when thinking about the right career for you, you need to take into account the following factors:

- your personality
- your preferences
- your values
- your talents and skills.

You could start by asking several people who know you well where they think your strengths, weaknesses and talents lie. You might not always agree with everything they say, but they might come up with something interesting you don't expect, or good points about yourself that you've forgotten.

Tutors at school and careers advisers can be very helpful for bouncing ideas off, and they can put you on the right path to find out reliable information. If you don't have any clue what sort of work you'd like to do, you could try some questionnaires and quizzes to identify sectors to research in greater detail – ask a careers adviser for ones such as the Kudos and Careerscape programmes. You can also try www.fasttomato.com, or fill in the Career Values Tool or the Skills and Interests Assessment at http://careersadvice.direct. gov.uk. You will then be able to:

- look at broad areas of work that might suit you
- narrow choices down into job sectors, and consider future career options, and then
- research specific job requirements, wages, the current job market and career prospects.

You can use Part 2 of this book for this part of your research. It will point you in the right direction so that you can find out more from official sources. You can also look at careers advice and labour market information on the following websites:

- http://careersadvice.direct.gov.uk/helpwithyourcareer
- www.connexions-direct.com/jobs4u
- www.sscalliance.org.

After all this, if you're fairly sure that you want to leave school and get a job or start an apprenticeship soon, turn to the next chapter. It will help you to make the right preparations and make the most of the opportunities available to you.

Chapter 3
Preparing to leave school

．．

If you're seriously thinking about leaving education soon, there are many things that you can do to improve your chances of career success in the future. By now, you will probably have some idea of the type of employment or work training that interests you. But be aware that there's much more to it than simply applying for jobs or apprenticeships.

Other people will be applying for the things you want too, so it's important to make the effort to stand out from the competition. The good news is that there are lots of ways you can give yourself that vital edge. To give yourself an advantage, you can:

- do plenty of research so that you know what you want, and where to find it
- work hard at school or college to get the best grades you can
- follow the news and gossip in the industries that interest you the most
- start some activities that will look good on an application form or CV
- build some contacts in any industry or organisation that you are interested in
- begin putting a CV or other record of your skills and talents together
- start searching for jobs or trainee vacancies before everyone else does
- take the time to learn a few interview and job application skills.

As you gather more information, you might end up changing your mind about what you want. You might also find that you need to change your plans. For example, you might find out that your dream job needs a special qualification, so you will have to decide whether to study for this, or start looking for a different kind of job. The more information and advice you can get at this stage, the better (see Chapter 2).

Leaving school: the law

○ If you live in England, Wales or Northern Ireland there is an official school-leaving date. This is the last Friday in June of the year of your 16th birthday. The law says that you can only start a full-time job after the last Friday in June, even if you turned 16 before this date.

○ In Scotland, there are two leaving dates, dependent on when you turn 16. If you are 16 between 1 March and 30 September you can leave on 31 May of that year. If you are 16 between 1 October and the following 28 February, then you can leave on the first day of the Christmas holidays.

Making your CV look good

Once you have a firm idea of the work that interests you, and what you would like to apply for, you should start some activities that will appeal to employers. If you haven't done this already, try some:

○ work experience
○ paid work
○ volunteering
○ positions of responsibility at school/college
○ after-school clubs and other activities.

Work experience

To see for yourself what a job's really like, apply for some work experience. It's best to arrange this with the help of your teachers/careers adviser at your school or college, rather than trying to organise it yourself. If your school isn't already offering what you want, keep them informed while you contact local businesses, check the local paper and business websites for opportunities, and ask around family and friends. Work experience is part of some courses in Year 10 or 11, including certain GCSEs and the newer Diploma. You might need to work in a business or organisation full time for one to three weeks, or spend one day per week in a workplace over a longer period.

Work experience will give you knowledge, confidence, and perhaps some new skills, but most importantly, it will allow you to decide if this is something you truly enjoy or not. Work experience can also help you build contacts in your chosen industry or organisation – these can be a perfect source of information, support, mentoring or even future employment. To find out more, do some research at:

○ www.direct.gov.uk/en/EducationAndLearning
○ www.placementsurvivalguide.com
○ www.need2know.co.uk/work/work_experience
○ www.work-experience.org/ncwe.rd/teenagers.jsp.

Paid work

Paid work could be evening or weekend work, or holiday jobs. It will bring in some cash, and you can learn lots of useful skills and prove that you are a reliable and employable person. Make a note of any work duties and responsibilities and add them to your CV.

Volunteering

There are many benefits of becoming a volunteer, and you can also make a contribution to your community. Volunteering shows commitment and enthusiasm, and makes you look caring and unselfish. In return for your time and effort you can meet lots of different people in different environments, try new things, make some achievements towards goals, and increase your self-esteem. To get started, go to:

- o   www.direct.gov.uk/en/YoungPeople/Workandcareers
- o   www.volunteering.org.uk
- o   http://vinspired.com
- o   www.dofe.org
- o   www.timebank.org.uk.

Other activities

There are several other supporting activities you can carry out to help your job applications. For example, you could do some charity fundraising, join a sports team or music group, or volunteer for responsibilities such as a team captain or class representative. If you have any talents or skills you can also try entering some competitions. Try to think about what employers might be looking for, such as ability to work in a team, sales skills, responsibility, creativity, competitiveness, or leadership skills. You will need to fit these activities around your studies, so pick carefully and don't take on too much.

Keeping up to date

It's helpful to follow what's happening at present in your chosen field of work. Start by searching for stories in the general news on TV and in the newspapers. You should also regularly read any major industry journals and visit the news sections of official websites. This can help you to learn more about the work that you could be doing, avoid problem areas, find new opportunities where there might be job vacancies, or look really smart at job interviews.

Starting to look for jobs or trainee vacancies

The old saying 'the early bird catches the worm' is true. If you start looking in plenty of time, you have a better chance of finding what you want. Also, if you apply quickly (and carefully) soon after a job or apprenticeship is advertised, it makes a good impression on an employer and shows them that you are keen to work for them.

Find out how to start putting together a CV and other records of your skills and talents in Chapter 4, where you can also learn about useful work search, and interview and job application skills. To look at ways to find and apply for apprenticeships and other work-based training, see Chapter 5.

Chapter 4
Choosing to get a job

∙∙

I f you've chosen to get a job, the information in this chapter will help you make a successful start in your search for work.

Hopefully by this stage you will have some broad idea of the kind of work you'd like to do (if not, take your time and go back through the steps described in Chapters 2 and 3, or look through the jobs directory in Part 2 for inspiration). The next step is to find and apply for all the jobs that you think are suitable for you.

You have to be well organised when you're looking for employment – some people even say that you should treat looking for a job as though the process is a job in itself. As with many other things in life, finding employment often needs some effort putting into it before things pay off, but there can also be an element of luck. Sometimes you're fortunate and a great job turns up quickly. At other times it can take a lot longer to find the right one.

Keeping good notes

It helps to create a job search folder on your computer so that you know where everything is, and have a record of whom you've contacted and when. It's also a good idea to have another (physical) file for paperwork, including letters to and from employers, and photocopies of any non-digital material that you've sent off with your applications. For example, at an interview you might be asked about something you put on your application form, and you'll need to be able to remember what you wrote.

The next step is to start putting together a basic CV (also known as a *curriculum vitae* or résumé), and finding some job vacancies.

Getting a CV together

Your CV is a formal document that you use to introduce yourself to an employer, to show them what you have to offer. It should help you 'market' yourself as a good worker, and make the employer like you and want to give you the job. Invest some time in creating a good CV and it will act as a successful advertisement for you.

Where to start

Think about the type of work that you really want to do and hope to apply for. Then try to get inside the employer's head and think about what they might be looking for in a person – all jobs need certain skills or talents, or personal qualities, and some need specific qualifications and experience. Your CV needs to show you have all this. It also needs to be clear and easy to understand. If you're making statements about yourself, think about ways that you can show evidence to the employer to back up these statements.

What to include

CVs can have different layouts, and the information doesn't have to be in this set order. You must always include your name and contact details and you should try to include:

- a summary of why you'd be good for the particular job
- your education history, qualifications and key skills
- your work history
- your hobbies, interests, out-of-school activities
- names and contact details of references.

Contact details

Your name, address, phone number and email address must be at the top of the document. Don't write 'CV' or 'curriculum vitae' at the top – the recruiters will know what a CV looks like so you don't need to state the obvious. Give the employer more than one way of contacting you. Use an email address that looks professional (chris.harris@pmail.com is far better than iluvJLS@supafan.co.uk). Make sure it's one that you check very regularly and won't forget the password for, because you don't want to miss out if you're offered an interview. Also make sure that the voicemail message on your phone is simple and professional too – don't have one that tells an employer that you're 'too busy partying right now to pick up the phone', for example.

An optional summary

The summary is sometimes called a 'personal profile'. This usually consists of two or three sentences that sum you up succinctly, so that a busy reader can find out the most important points about you in a few seconds. Keep it upbeat and positive. You might want to mention your career aims in this area of your CV.

Education history, qualifications and skills

If you're still at school, this section will be bigger than your work history section. Say which schools you've been to, including the years that you started and finished. Include all your qualifications, and predicted grades. Also include key skills that you've picked up at school, and any personal achievements. If the job you want needs certain subjects, write more about those important subjects. Say which parts of these subjects you like the best, or perform best at. Employers will probably also want to know about your computer skills, so mention all the software programs you have experience of using. Employers usually need you to have good basic skills in English and maths too. To save space and keep things simple, use subheadings and bullet points for some of your information.

Work history
You won't be expected to have a full-time work history if you haven't left education yet. However, this is a great opportunity to write about part-time jobs, holiday jobs, helping out with your family's business, work experience, volunteer work or charity fundraising. Include the names of the employers and the dates that you worked, and describe what your responsibilities and duties were.

Show that you are willing to work and learn, that you are reliable and have gained some useful skills. For example, don't just say you sell ice cream in a kiosk by the beach at the weekend – explain that you turn up early every Saturday morning, are good at handling money, understand food safety laws, know about the importance of customer service, and are trusted to lock up at the end of the day – that will give the employer a much better picture. Can you work well under pressure, manage time well, train or supervise others, deal with difficult people, or pick up new skills quickly? Tell an employer about this in the Work section of your CV.

Other relevant information
Include your hobbies, interests, clubs you're part of, and out-of-school interests, but only those that are likely to make a good impression on the employer. It's a chance to show a bit more about your personality, but keep it simple. So don't give a long list of hobbies, just stick to two or three, and remember that 'reading', 'watching TV' and 'socialising' can look a bit boring. Try to strike a balance between looking like an interesting person who will be an asset to the organisation and looking so individual that you won't fit in with the other employees.

If the job you're going for needs someone who works well in a team, and you're part of the football or hockey team, or part of a band or a charity work group do mention that. To show responsibility or leadership, if you are the captain of a team, a class representative, a leader in the Guides, or if you have set some group or scheme up, you should mention that too. To show warmth and compassion, tell the employer if you do volunteer work or fundraising, or have trained as a first-aider, etc. If you have joined a scheme, such as the Duke of Edinburgh's Award or Young Enterprise, or won any prizes, make sure you write about them in this section, as these are big achievements.

References
Some employers need two references, others ask for three or more. Ask people who know you, and who are respected by others, if they are willing to give you a reference

before you put their names down. You can't ask family members, but teachers, employers or people you volunteer for or have done work experience for would be ideal. Pick people who you think will say that you have a pleasant personality and a healthy attitude towards work, and include their contact details on your CV.

Useful resources for CV writing

If you want to write the best CV you can, get lots of extra help with it.

- Your school or college might have some factsheets or offer a CV-checking service.

- You can also get help from careers advice tutors and Connexions advisers.

- There are some useful websites, such as:
  - http://careersadvice.direct.gov.uk/helpwithyourcareer/writecv/
  - http://www.kent.ac.uk/careers/cv.htm
  - http://www.howtobooks.co.uk/employment/cvs/

- You could also borrow or buy a book about how to write a CV, such as *You're Hired! How to Write a Brilliant CV* by Corinne Mills (Trotman, £9.99), *Brilliant CV: What Employers Want to See and How to Say it* by Dr Jim Bright and Joanne Earl (Prentice Hall, £9.99) or *The CV Book: Your Definitive Guide to Writing the Perfect CV* by James Innes (Prentice Hall, £9.99).

Extra tips for writing a successful CV

- Use a clear format.
- Get to the point quickly – make it punchy.
- Give the employer what they've asked for.
- Don't tell lies.
- Double-check everything.
- Take care when printing out a CV.
- Alter your CV to fit every job you apply for.

Using a clear format

Most employers will want to see a CV that's two pages long, clearly laid out, and easy to read and understand. Some of the resources mentioned in the box above have several examples of what attractive CVs look like. Have a look at them to get a few pointers and ideas. Use a plain, simple font because this is easiest to read, and avoid anything that looks too fussy or fancy. Keep the point size of your text to 12, or perhaps 10. Anything else will look too large or be too small to read. Set the font colour to black, and don't add lots of different colours. It's best not to include any pictures unless you have been asked for them.

Use clear subheadings to break up the different parts of your text, and put in as much relevant information as you can without making the pages look too overcrowded. Remember to leave some white space between each section as this will make your text more easy and pleasant to read.

Making it punchy

If there are, say, 500 applications for a particular job, it is very unlikely that the recruiting person or team is going to read through every word of every CV that arrives. They simply do not have the time for this, and might only spend a few seconds briefly scanning the first page. A CV that's full of waffle, hard to read or full of spelling mistakes is likely to go straight in the bin without a second thought. Remember to keep your CV short and snappy, and put the most important information first — getting straight to the point can really help you stand out from the competition. Use lots of dynamic language too, to give your CV the right tone; you can use words and phrases such as 'completed', 'created', 'set up', 'ran', 'designed', and 'organised'. The resources given above will have more details about this.

Do as they ask

When an employer asks for a specific format in a CV, you must give them *exactly* what they've asked for. If they ask you to send a two-page Word file as an attachment to an email then do exactly that. It will only make them annoyed if you send them a one-page CV or a link to your website instead, for example. Try to see it from their point of view: they're busy people who don't have time to fill in the gaps on a one-page CV or go looking for important details that are buried somewhere on a large website. Make it easy for them to do their job.

Don't tell lies

However tempted you might be to tell a few fibs to make your CV stand out from the rest on the pile, don't give in to the temptation to tell an outright lie about anything. It's easy to get tripped up by an interviewer, and if they find that you've abused their trust at that stage then you're unlikely to get offered the job. People have also been sacked from their dream jobs after lies on their CVs came to light, so ask yourself, is it really worth the risk? Employers are getting more and more sophisticated at spotting dishonest applications, and bigger firms even hire private agencies to check facts when they're recruiting. By all means play up your good points and play down anything you think might be seen negatively, but don't lie.

Double-check it

Once you've created your basic CV, check it, check it again, and then check it again. Then get other trustworthy people to check it for you, especially if your grammar and spelling sometimes need a little extra help. This might sound a bit over the top, but it is worth all the effort in the long run. Ask yourself the following questions.

- Are my contact details correct?
- Is the layout clear and easy to read?
- Is the spelling perfect?
- Does it show me in a good light?
- Does it contain good examples of my skills, experience or talent?
- Can it give an employer a good idea of me in a few seconds?

Once you're happy, save the document and make a couple of paper copies. Remember to back the file up too, in case of computer problems.

What do employers really want?

Whatever employers say they want in their job advertisements, most of them are also looking for a few universal things. When you're putting a CV together, filling in an application form or sitting in an interview, remember that they probably want someone who:

- turns up on time and takes the job seriously

- is trustworthy, especially with money or property

- can use everyday computer software

- can follow health and safety instructions

- is able to take the initiative and solve problems

- is polite to customers, even under pressure

- generally 'fits in' with the rest of the employees.

Don't be scared to mention any of these 'unwritten' things that they might want – it certainly won't harm your chances, and it might help you a lot.

Printing your CV

Although most employers now ask you to send your CV as an electronic file in an email attachment, a few might want you to post them a copy. If that's the case, use only white or off-white paper and make sure that it isn't creased, marked or smudged. The employer will probably keep all the applications in a pile before looking through them – yours will stand out best if it hasn't been folded several times, and if it hasn't been printed on the cheapest, thinnest paper. If possible, send it in an A4-sized envelope so you don't have to fold it at all. A first class stamp makes an impression too – that you're keen for it to arrive quickly.

'Tailoring' your CV

Once you've created a basic CV and saved the original copy, you are free to tailor it so that it's the best fit for each job you apply for. Some employers ask for specific skills or experience in their advertisements, so you can add more detail to those parts of your CV, and perhaps have less detail in other parts to compensate. You can also move different sections around so that the most important information for that employer is nearer the start of the document, and has the most impact. It's a good idea to alter your CV for every new position you apply for – this way you can make yourself most appealing to specific recruiters, and it will also increase your chances of success.

What do YOU want from an employer?

Obviously when you're looking for work, you need to persuade the employer that you're the right person for the job. It's also useful to take a step back and decide whether they're the right people to employ you. By this stage you've probably put a lot of thought into the type of work you want, and the broad area of employment you're most interested in. There might only be one main company nearby that offers those jobs, but if you have a choice of organisations then try to think about the following.

- **Size**. Do you want to work somewhere large, where there might be specialised roles you could grow into? Or do you want to work somewhere smaller, where you might have to do lots of different tasks at the same time? Do you want to work somewhere that has a local, national or international base?

- **Structure**. Would you be happier working in a place that's fairly informal, or would you like something with a clear management structure and more obvious paths for promotion?

- **Culture**. What kind of atmosphere would you prefer to work in? While the culture of an organisation might be influenced by its size and structure, that isn't the whole story. The culture can be professional, friendly, strict, fun-loving, laid-back, competitive, adrenaline-fuelled, gossipy, traditional, or creative. The culture of an employer might be difficult to work out, but you might get some idea from their promotional materials or by talking to people who work there.

- **Prospects**. Once you've settled into a job, what are the career prospects like? Are there formal or informal opportunities to learn new skills and gain valuable experience? Is there a clear career path? Will you need to gain extra qualifications to get a promotion? While you might be happy in a new job to begin with, most people need to have some new challenges after a while, and to feel a sense of progress.

Once you have a clear idea of what you want from a job, and from an organisation, it's time to start hunting for work.

Where to look for work

There are official and unofficial ways to find work, and to increase your chances of finding the job that you would love to do, you should try everything. Look for official job advertisements here:

- school/college notice boards or careers offices
- your local Connexions Centre (visit www.connexions-direct.com and click on 'Local Services' for the address)
- your local Job Centre (look in the phone book for the address)
- http://jobseekers.direct.gov.uk
- local and national newspapers and magazines, and their websites
- commercial job websites such as www.jobserve.co.uk, www.totaljobs.com, www.monster.co.uk, www.fish4jobs.co.uk, www.workthing.com
- local shop windows (mostly for casual work)
- recruitment agencies.

You can also try some less 'official' routes, which can be effective:

- ask around all your family and friends, neighbours, etc.
- write to people you've done work experience for in the past
- ask at your school or college whether they have good links with any local employers
- research businesses in the field you're interested in, and search their websites for job openings
- if companies you've researched are not advertising any vacancies at the moment, you can still call them up, speak to someone in the human resources department, send them a CV to keep on file, and contact them again from time to time
- take your CV and personally hand it in to businesses around town.

It can be a lot of hard work, and you need to try lots of different tactics. You also need to keep going and not give up, even if at times you might feel discouraged.

When you see an advertisement you like

Read the ad very carefully – what is the deadline date that the employer has given, and are you entitled to apply for it? Do not waste their time or your own if they are insisting on a particular qualification that you don't have. What are they asking you to send in? Send them exactly what they have asked for, whether that's a CV, a letter, an application form or a portfolio. Send your application off quickly, as this makes you look keen and gives them the best impression. Keep a copy of your application and the job ad in your job search folder.

How to apply

The application process differs from job to job. You might be asked for any of the following, in any combination:

- your CV
- a covering letter/email

o   an application form
o   examples of previous work, or portfolio.

We've already looked at CVs, and how you should slightly alter them to fit each job you are applying for. Let's look at the other documents now.

The covering letter/email

The covering letter is a simple but important letter (or email) that you send in with your CV. It's the first thing that the employer's going to look at, so make sure that you make the right kind of impression. Include your name at the bottom of the letter and your contact details at the top. Introduce yourself politely, say where you saw their job advertised, and very briefly mention why the job sounds interesting and why you would be a good person for the job. If possible, briefly mention one or two of the facts from your CV to show that you have the right experience or attitude – this should make them look at your CV more carefully after they've finished reading your letter. You can also include a small amount of information that's not on your CV, if it's a good fit for this job.

Keep your letter or email fairly short, around three paragraphs, or one side of A4 paper. Check it carefully for mistakes such as spelling and grammar, and if you're writing to a particular person always make sure you spell their name correctly. Write this letter neatly using a word processor, and if they've asked for a printed copy, print it off using black ink onto good quality paper. More rarely, you might be asked to send a handwritten letter – if that's the case, write it out in rough first onto scrap paper and get the words right, then use your best handwriting on good quality paper for the final version. Make sure there are no mistakes, fingerprints, creases or smudged ink, and write your letter away from people who are eating, drinking or smoking. Make photocopies of your handwritten letter and keep them in a safe place, or scan them and save them in your job search folder.

Application forms

Employers and employment agencies often ask people to fill in application forms because they want specific information, and it helps them to compare candidates more easily. Take your time when filling in these forms – first read all the instructions you're given. Make sure you give them the right information, with good spelling and grammar. Get someone you trust to help you check what you've written, to make sure there are no mistakes and that you've presented yourself as well as possible.

If you don't know how to fill in a section of the form, ask for help from a teacher at school or a careers counsellor. Try not to leave any section blank unless the form's instructions say it's okay to do that. Most application forms are digital documents, so once you're happy with the way you've filled it in you can save a copy for yourself and then email it. If you're asked to fill in a paper form, take a few photocopies of it first and practise filling in the photocopies until you've got it looking just right. Then fill in the real form very carefully using your best handwriting, making sure there are no mistakes or smudges.

Make photocopies of this form for yourself so you can read through the form to help you prepare if you are invited to an interview.

Examples of work

Sometimes an employer will ask you for examples of other work you have done. This collection is sometimes called a portfolio, and is more common for jobs where you need to show how creative you are. It depends on the job, as the employer might want to see samples of anything from photographs you've taken, to artwork you've created, articles or stories you've written, furniture you've built, or hair and make-up looks you've designed. You need to create a good impact, so only use examples of your best work.

For most jobs, it's best to send high quality copies of your work, rather than the originals, just in case they get lost in the post and can never be replaced. You can also put examples on a website and give the employer the link to it. If they want the original copies, take them to the employer in person or send them by registered post or a reliable courier. Make sure that you have included your return postal details with your portfolio in case it is mislaid or lost.

Sending off your application

Whatever you've been asked to send in, give it one last check through and get it to the employer before the deadline they have set. Make sure you've sent them everything they've asked for, and make a note of when you posted or emailed it. If you're sending paperwork in the post, use good quality envelopes that are big enough to put the papers in without folding them. Post the applications first class, using the right postage for the size of the envelope, so they arrive quickly.

What next after the applications?

After you've sent off your application, be prepared to wait for a while before the employer contacts you. This is often the most difficult part of the application process, especially if it's a job you are really interested in, or you need to start earning some money. It's okay to call the employer once to make sure that your application has arrived safely, because the postal system and email servers are not perfect, but keep the call short and polite. Try to keep yourself busy while you're waiting by looking and applying for more jobs.

Following up

If you haven't heard back from the employer a short time after their applications deadline has closed, don't jump to any conclusions. They might be too busy to get back to you straight away, or something might have been lost in the post, for example. After a reasonable amount of time has passed, follow up with them via email or phone to find out what is happening. Be mentally prepared for what might happen next: you might be rejected, asked to send more information, asked to attend an interview or test, or your email might go unanswered. Some employers do not take the time to contact the people they reject, but there is no harm in double-checking the status of your application with them, just in case. A few recruiters are offhand or unhelpful to applicants, but if that happens do try to show good manners, even if you are upset — you never know who that recruiter might talk to and some industries are 'small worlds'.

The next stage of the application process
By now you will be facing one of three main possibilities:

1. rejection
2. an invitation to attend an interview
3. an invitation to attend testing (see box below).

It is quite common to get several rejections before you find a job, and it is rare to be employed straight after you've started applying. Rejection is not a pleasant feeling, but you do have to pick yourself up afterwards and start looking for other job opportunities. If you're getting many rejections, talk to someone about why that might be happening — there could simply be a lot of competition for those jobs, or you might need to change what you're applying for, or the way you're applying for it.

If you're offered an interview or asked to attend a test then congratulations, you're one big step closer to getting work. Contact the employer immediately to confirm that you will be attending this meeting.

Attending testing

Some companies might ask you to fill out personality questionnaires, complete tests in person or online, or attend an assessment centre. How can you improve your chances?

o Find out well in advance what type of tests these will be, and think about how you can show the employer that you have what they're looking for.

o Speak to a careers tutor or Connexions adviser to see whether there's any extra study that you can do to prepare for these types of test.

o If you are attending in person, turn up on time and be smartly dressed and polite. Treat it like a formal interview (see below).

Preparing for an interview
It's helpful to have a quick checklist when you're preparing for interviews. In general it should run as follows:

1. confirm your attendance with the employer
2. note times and places in your diary
3. re-read their job advertisement
4. re-read what you've sent to them

5. check the address of the interview place
6. ask about the format of the interview
7. find out more about the company
8. think about questions they might ask you
9. prepare your questions for them
10. smarten up your appearance
11. pack your bag
12. plan your journey.

Go back, check, think

Once you've confirmed that you will be attending an interview, go back to the original advertisement and have a long look at it. Remind yourself what they're looking for, and also have another look at everything you've sent to them so far. If you've kept good notes and back-ups, this information should all be at your fingertips. Then double check the address of the interview, and think about personal safety. For example, if you're applying for an office-based job in the middle of town then an interview at a non-work location (such as a café or bar) or a remote place should make you suspicious. Never agree to get into a car with a stranger or let them come to your home to meet you.

Questions, questions

Check with the employer about the form that the interview will take. Find out what you need to bring, how many people will be interviewing you, how long it will last, and whether there will be any tests on the day. Then find out everything you can about the company if you haven't done that already – where they operate, what their values are, their size, and so on. Read any materials the company has sent to you, and check its website too. This background information will make you look like a serious candidate at the interview, because you've made the effort to study it. It will also help you to think of one or two good questions to ask the interviewers.

You should also have a think about common questions that an interviewer might ask you – a careers officer or Connexions adviser might be able to help you with this, or you could read a book about interview techniques (see the useful resources on p. 31).

If you've never been to an interview before, your school or college might be able to help you with a mock interview so that you can practise your interview skills. The experience will give you some self-confidence, and make the process less stressful when you turn up at the real interview. It's also helpful to keep an eye on the general news in the run-up to an interview – you might be asked questions about a news story that relates to your potential employer's field of work.

Smarten up

Even if the job you want doesn't need you to dress smartly, make an effort with your appearance when you go to the interview.

- It's always better to be a little too smartly dressed rather than a little too casually dressed. Show the employer that you take them seriously and yourself seriously.
- If possible, find out what people who work there wear, and dress a little like them if you can – it will make you look like you already work there.
- Wear clothes that are clean and ironed, but don't wear footwear that's completely brand new on the day in case it's uncomfortable.
- Clean your shoes the night before, and make sure you're showered and wearing an effective deodorant on the day.
- Women should keep make-up light, and everyone should avoid wearing flashy jewellery.

The day before your interview

Work out your route to get from your home to the interview. Allow plenty of extra time in case there are problems with traffic or public transport, and plan to arrive at least 10 minutes early. The night before the interview, print out a map or other directions and put them in your bag along with anything else you might need for the interview, including a pen, copies of your CV and the application form, and your questions. Make sure you have the employer's contact telephone number with you in case you are delayed and need to call ahead. Set out your clothes for the next day before you go to bed so you aren't rushed the next morning. Try to get an early night so you're well rested, and double-check that you've set your alarm clock to the correct time.

On the day

Get up early, make sure you have some breakfast to help you concentrate, and leave the house on time.

Telephone interviews

Some employers might ask you to do a telephone interview, where you don't need to go in to their offices. If you're invited to one of these, take it seriously and treat it like a formal interview (see below).

- If the time has been arranged in advance, make sure you're in a place where there's as little background noise as possible and you won't be interrupted.
- The main advantage of a phone interview is that you can have all your records in front of you to refer to, so set these out before the interview begins.
- Don't drink, smoke or chew gum while talking on the phone, and try to sit up straight to make your voice sound clear and professional.
- Let the interviewer finish speaking before you start talking, and take your time to think before answering any questions.
- At the end of the interview say thank-you and goodbye, and let them be the first person to hang up the phone.

Doing well at an interview

First impressions do count, so:

- arrive in good time, about 10 to 15 minutes early
- go to the toilet to freshen up and check your appearance
- wipe your hands on a tissue if they sweat when you're nervous
- smile, look the interviewers in the eye, and give them a firm handshake
- wait to be asked to sit down
- sit up straight and try to look confident and interested
- if you feel a bit nervous, breathe slowly and deeply.

Then the interviewers will start asking you their questions.

- Think about your answer for a moment, rather than blurting something out quickly.
- If you don't understand a question, ask the interviewer to explain what they mean.
- Try not to give one or two word answers, make it one or two sentences at least, and try to back your comments up with examples of personal experience.
- Make an effort to sound positive and professional, even if you are being asked to talk about negative things — it's good to talk about overcoming obstacles or learning from experience.
- Remember to think about your body language at the same time, and keep eye contact with the person who has asked you the question.

Towards the end of the interview, you might be given the chance to ask questions about the company.

- Ask your prepared questions, or ask about something that might have struck you during the interview.
- Questions about prospects for learning on the job and career progression will make you look keen and like someone who is thinking about working for the organisation in the long term.
- Keep it to two or three questions if you can.

At the end of the interview:

- stand up when the interviewers stand up
- shake hands and say thank-you.

Useful resources for interviews

Most commercial job websites have free articles with tips on how to do well in an interview. You can also get advice from careersadvice.direct.gov.uk and thesite.org.

It's worth reading a book about interview techniques too, such as *You're Hired! Interview: Tips and Techniques for a Brilliant Interview* by Judi James (Trotman, £9.99), *Perfect Interview* by Max Eggert (Random House, £7.99), *Brilliant Interview: What Employers Want to Hear and How to Say it* by Ros Jay (Prentice Hall, £9.99), or *The Interview Book: Your Definitive Guide to the Perfect Interview Technique* by James Innes (Prentice Hall, £9.99).

What next after the interview?

You should hear back from the organisation within a few days. If they don't contact you, follow up with a polite phone call to ask about their decision. They might:

- offer you the job
- offer you a different job
- ask for more information or a second interview
- send a rejection letter or email.

Job offers

If you're offered the job, make sure you know what salary and benefits the employer is proposing, and ask about your contract and starting dates. Read the contract carefully. If there's anything in it that you're not sure about always ask the employer, a careers tutor or a Connexions adviser for help. If you don't think they are offering enough money, you could ask for more pay or better benefits at this stage, but do be prepared for them to say no. If you decide to take the offer, sign and return the contract and any other paperwork they send you. Congratulations – you are now an employee!

Alternative offers

Sometimes an employer might offer you a different type of work, or a job in another department that they think you'd be better suited to. Get as much information as you can about this alternative work before making any decision, and ask as many questions as you need to.

Second interviews

You might be called in for a second interview. Prepare as well for the second interview as you did for the first. Stay positive too, you're still in the running for the job, even if it feels like another hurdle for you to jump.

Rejection

Sadly, not everyone who is interviewed will be given a job. If you're rejected at this stage in the recruitment process, it is usually worth contacting the employer and politely asking for some feedback. Listen carefully to the feedback and decide whether you could make any changes to do better at your next interview.

What if you can't find what you want?

Sometimes, no matter how hard you try, it can be difficult to find interesting employment in the area that you want to work in. What are your options if this happens?

- Keep searching for your ideal job, and increase your efforts using all the search and application techniques mentioned in this chapter (if you find yourself unemployed, see page 211 of this book for more help).
- Take a different job in the field you like the look of, and hope that you can work your way up into the job you really want.
- Broaden your job search into different fields. If you're unsure about which way to go, speak to careers advisers, Connexions advisers, schoolteachers and college tutors, and any wise relatives you might have.
- Take a 'stop-gap' job – any job you can find to get some wages coming in – then carry on your job search for your ideal job while you're working.
- Apply for short-term work, or temporary or casual jobs. 'Temp' jobs can sometimes lead on to permanent job offers, so you could start by looking for temp work in the fields that interest you the most.
- Apply for paid or unpaid work experience. If you make a good impression it might lead on to a job offer, although there is no guarantee of this. You will have to weigh up all the pros and cons and decide for yourself whether it's worth the risk.
- Go back to school or college and study practical or academic subjects. While it might not be your first choice, at least you can get some funding and useful qualifications from the experience, and you should have lots of resources around that you can make use of.
- Look at apprenticeships and other work-based training that's being offered in your local area. This is covered in Chapter 5.

Chapter 5

Apprenticeships and jobs with training

This chapter covers apprenticeships and jobs with training which lead to official, recognised qualifications that are part of the National Framework. They allow you to earn and learn at the same time. Over time, people who have apprenticeship qualifications tend to earn a lot more than people with no qualifications.

Apprenticeships

Apprenticeships are best for young people who already have quite a firm idea of the type of work they want to do. It's important to research them carefully and make sure that you're committed to the idea before applying for one. Apprenticeships for school leavers are mainly available at two levels:

- o apprenticeships: Level 2 (equivalent to five GCSEs at grade C and above)
- o advanced apprenticeships: Level 3 (equivalent to two A levels).

Most apprenticeships lead to National Vocational Qualifications (NVQs) or Scottish Vocational Qualifications (SVQs) as their recognised official qualifications, usually at Level 2 or Level 3. On top of NVQs/SVQs, you can also gain:

- o Key Skills qualifications (e.g. using technology, or problem solving)
- o Technical certificates such as BTECs or City & Guilds Progression Awards
- o Other new vocational qualifications that will be available as part of the Qualifications and Credit Framework (QCF) from the end of 2010.

There are also some *higher apprenticeships* available to over-16s. You are expected to work towards work-based learning qualifications such as NVQ Level 4 or, in some cases, a knowledge-based qualification such as a foundation degree.

Apprenticeships can take between one and four years to complete, depending on what you apply for. You sign up with a specific employer, and earn a wage while you're working and learning. The employer will help you to gain work experience, build up your skills and gain officially recognised qualifications. There are over 190 different apprenticeship roles available, in over 80 industry sectors – what's on offer can vary from area to area depending on the businesses near where you live.

Apprenticeships: wages

o During an apprenticeship you can expect to be paid at least £95 per week, unless you work in agriculture, which can pay less.

o If you are aged 16–18 years, the National Apprenticeship Service gives money to your employer, who then pays this to you as wages.

o You are not automatically entitled to receive the minimum wage.

o If you are over 16, you have to pay tax if you earn over a certain amount and national insurance (to learn more about this, see p. 209).

o Official statistics suggest that the average apprentice takes home around £170 per week, with highest rates around £210 per week.

o As you gain more experience and skills, your apprenticeship employer might start to pay you a higher wage.

Training

Most training takes place in the workplace. You also spend time off the job with a training provider – often a local college or a specialist work-based training organisation – studying for vocational qualifications. Off-the-job training can take place on a day-release basis or you might be given a number of days off work in a block.

The amount of time spent on training away from the workplace varies according to the type of apprenticeship. According to Apprenticeships.org.uk this could be anything from one day every other fortnight to two days every week.

'Not everybody learns best in a classroom environment – we all know someone like that. We've come across hundreds of apprentices who have gone on to be incredibly successful in their chosen careers. The real life work experience they gained as an apprentice is something that future employers really value.

'Apprenticeships lead to nationally recognised qualifications, social skills and experience in their chosen field. Apprenticeships lead to a bright future.'

Simon Waugh, Chief Executive of the National Apprenticeships Service

---

What are your apprenticeship options?

This information applies to young people living in England. For the other UK countries, see page 35. To apply for any apprenticeship you must be:

- over the age of 16
- living in England
- not in full-time education.

There might be different extra entry requirements for apprenticeships depending on the occupational sector and type of apprenticeship you are applying for. Depending on your grades in GCSE Maths and English, you might need to take literacy and numeracy tests.

In England, apprenticeships are divided into 10 main industry types:

- agriculture, horticulture and animal care
- arts, media and publishing
- business, administration and law
- construction, planning and the built environment
- education and training
- engineering and manufacturing technologies
- health, public services and care
- information and communication technology
- leisure, travel and tourism
- retail and commercial enterprise.

Each one is split into several sub-sections. To find out more, visit www.apprenticeships.org. uk and look at the 'Types of Apprenticeships' section.

Northern Ireland, Scotland and Wales

Apprenticeships are slightly different outside England. For full information about what's on offer and how to apply, try these resources:

- **Northern Ireland**: has Apprenticeships (NI). Try www.delni.gov.uk/apprenticeships_flyer.pdf and www.apprenticeshipsNI.info

- **Scotland**: has Modern Apprenticeships. Try http://www.careers-scotland.org.uk/Education/Training/ModernApprenticeship.asp

- **Wales**: has Apprenticeships and Training. Try http://new.careerswales.com/16to19/server.php?show=nav.4749

What's expected of you

Apprenticeships are not an easy option. You have to be prepared to work hard, be professional, and juggle work with studying. You also need to:

- make an effort to work well as part of a team
- turn up for your contracted hours
- be prepared to work well on your own

- o be able to use your own initiative sometimes
- o pass any assessments or exams.

What you can expect from your employer

Your employer must:

- o pay you regular wages
- o give you paid holiday time
- o provide quality on-the-job training with skilled staff
- o give you opportunities to learn job-specific skills
- o allow time off (usually day-release) for training
- o monitor and evaluate your work and learning
- o give you a safe place to do your job.

Holiday and benefits

- o Employed apprentices get at least 20 days' paid holiday per year, plus all bank holidays.

- o You should also receive the same benefits as the other company employees, e.g. access to a subsidised canteen or fitness facilities, pension contributions, or other schemes.

How to find apprenticeships

You can search for apprenticeships in a number of ways:

- o your local 14–19 Online Prospectus (http://yp.direct.gov.uk/14-19prospectus)
- o the Vacancy Matching Service at www.apprenticeships.org.uk
- o careers advice person or notice boards at your school or college
- o contacting local employers directly.

Signing up for an apprenticeship is quite a commitment, so it's not something anyone should rush straight into. Most people start by looking for apprenticeships in specific career sectors after first researching these different job areas. Once you've found an apprenticeship you like the look of, research it some more. Find out about the entry requirements and career prospects, and call potential employers for more information if needed.

Some apprenticeships are very popular and there can be a lot of competition for places. At the moment, among the most popular apprenticeships are engineering, business administration, construction and hospitality. If you're thinking about one of these, take extra time to make your application look as good as possible. Also think about getting some relevant work experience to increase your chances.

How to apply

You can search and apply for apprenticeships in England using www.apprenticeships.org. uk, the national apprenticeships website. To get started, register with the site, and provide a contact telephone number and a plain, professional-sounding email address. Remember that this is a job application, as well as an application for training.

Important points to note
- Keep a note of all your searches and applications.
- Keep a note of your email login details – don't lose them!
- When you find a job advert you like, read it carefully to make sure you have the skills or experience the employer is asking for.
- Make sure you use good spelling, punctuation and grammar in your application.
- List all your qualifications, including predicted grades.
- If there are extra questions, this is your chance to shine – write well, and make yourself sound like the best person for the job.
- Check back regularly to track the progress of your applications.

After the application

The selection process for an apprenticeship is the same as any other job application process. You might have one or more interviews with the employer, and in some cases, tests, to see whether you are the right person for the role. To give yourself the best possible chance at an interview, see Chapter 4.

If your application is successful, you will be given a work contract to sign. Read it carefully, because it is legally binding. For more advice about contracts, see page 207.

Jobs with training

There are also some jobs with training that are not offered through the apprenticeships route. These are sometimes called 'traineeships' or 'trainee vacancies', or the training might be mentioned in the job ad. Always make sure that the training is genuinely available and that it leads to an official qualification – read the small print of advertisements and contracts, and check with the education provider. Research the qualification that's being offered as well, to see how much use it will be to you in your future career.

Part 2

Directory of Jobs
(or Job families)

Contents and introduction

This directory looks at the employment opportunities that are open to school leavers: full-time jobs, apprenticeships and training posts. A wide range of jobs have been categorised into 'families' of broad employment sectors, and then the different job opportunities within each sector are described using brief job profiles. These tell you about the qualifications, skills and personal qualities needed to do well in a particular type of work and look at job prospects for the future. The job profiles include the contact details of official bodies that can provide extra advice about what qualifications and skills you need, how to arrange work experience, and what the work is like.

You'll also find case studies of interviews with young people who are working or training in different sectors, sharing their first-hand experiences. Contact details for all of the UK sector skills councils are given in Chapter 7 in Part 3, to give you a full overview. It has not been possible to include some of the less common types of job in this directory for reasons of space, but there are suggestions for extra jobs to research, and the resources to find out more about those careers are listed in Chapter 7.

In this part of the book you can look up details of a range of occupations from the following job sectors:

- administration, business, office work and financial services
- building and construction

- catering and hospitality
- computers and information technology (IT)
- design, arts and crafts
- education and training
- engineering, manufacturing and production
- environment, animals and plants
- healthcare
- languages, information and culture
- legal and political services
- leisure, sport and tourism
- marketing, advertising, media, print and publishing
- performing arts
- personal and cleaning services, including hair and beauty
- retail, sales and customer services
- science, mathematics and statistics
- security and the armed forces
- social work and counselling services
- transport and logistics.

Key to symbols (entry levels)

 = Qualifications not always needed

 = Apprenticeship

 = Advanced apprenticeship

 = Higher apprenticeship

 = Trainee posts offered

Family 1

Administration, business, office work and financial services

- -

Over four million people are involved in administration, business and office work in the UK, and just under one million people work in financial services. Every organisation needs administrative staff to keep operating, and there are many diverse types of job in the business and finance sectors.

These are mainly office-based jobs, and many of them need you to be good with figures or excellent at organising yourself and others. Most of these jobs need an eye for detail, whether that's arranging things for others, looking at health and safety, or writing complicated reports or keeping spreadsheets updated. People new to these jobs tend to start by working for businesses and other organisations. However, some people working in the business and financial services might become self-employed after gaining experience.

It's possible to go in at entry level and work your way up in many of these types of work. In the financial services, for example, there are opportunities to take night classes while you are working to gain a range of qualifications that can improve your career prospects. Many employers run their own training schemes and have opportunities to progress.

Jobs and contacts

Accounting technician

Collecting, checking and reporting on different types of financial information

Accounting technicians have varying roles in different organisations, but they are all responsible for monitoring financial processes, and maintaining and checking financial records. They might work in the areas of company expenditure, invoicing, tax returns or payroll. They are expected to collect and analyse data, and write reports.

Pros and cons

o You usually have a standard working week.
o You work in a team environment.
o There is a clear structure for promotion in many organisations.
o Some tasks can be repetitive or boring.

You

o Good head for numbers and an interest in finance.
o Strong IT skills, including an understanding of how to use spreadsheets and databases.
o Methodical and analytical.
o Able to communicate well verbally and in writing.

Entry/learning

o There are no set academic entry requirements for this type of work, but GCSEs in Maths and English are very useful.
o Apprenticeships might be available.
o Many people in this type of work study part time to gain accountancy qualifications from the Association of Accounting Technicians or the Association of Chartered Certified Accountants.

Money

Trainees often start on salaries of around £11,000–£14,000 per year.

Career progress

With experience and qualifications, technicians can earn £13,000–£29,000 per year. Some people train to become finance directors, management accountants or chartered accountants, although this can take some years and many exams need to be passed.

Association of Accounting Technicians www.aat.org.uk/yourbigfuture
Association of Chartered Certified Accountantws www.acca.co.uk

---

Administrative assistant

Providing general administrative support to staff in an office or department

The work includes dealing with internal and external correspondence, managing stationery supplies, answering the telephone, filing, updating electronic data, word processing, printing and photocopying. Jobs are available in all sectors, including business, charities and healthcare.

Pros and cons
- You usually have a standard working week.
- You will get an opportunity to learn many transferable skills, such as time and people management, customer service and software skills.
- Some tasks might be repetitive.

You
- An interest in business.
- Good at managing your time and workload.
- Excellent communication skills.
- Numeracy and IT skills.

Entry/learning
- There are no fixed entry requirements for this work, but some employers will ask for certain GCSEs or higher-level qualifications.
- Work experience in an office environment can be very helpful.
- Most training is on the job.
- You can gain NVQs and other qualifications in business administration.

Money
Starting salaries can be around £15,000 per year, with less for apprenticeships.

Career progress
You can earn up to £25,000+ per year with experience. It is possible to move into supervisory or management roles, or become a personal assistant (see p. 47). The work can give the person a thorough overview of how a company operates, so the role can lead into jobs in different areas of the same business too.

Council for Administration Careers www.breakinto.biz

Bank cashier/customer adviser

Dealing with bank or building society customers in person or over the telephone

Cashiers and advisers are the first point of contact for a bank or building society's customers, and they work in branches or in contact centres. They deal with requests, enquiries and complaints, including paying in or withdrawing money, giving advice on and selling their employer's products and services.

Pros and cons
- Branches tend to have standard working hours, but some are open on Saturdays.
- Some contact centres are open 24 hours a day, so there can be shift work.

○ The job market in this area is very competitive.
○ The training is structured with promotion opportunities.

You

○ Good customer service skills.
○ Good at maths and IT.
○ Work well in a team and on your own initiative.
○ Able to remain calm under pressure.

Entry/learning

○ Many employers ask for a minimum of four GCSEs (grades A–C), including Maths and English.
○ Apprenticeships are available.
○ Most training is on the job, often with highly structured programmes.
○ You can also study part time for a variety of qualifications from City & Guilds, IFS, BTEC and more. See www.fssc.org.uk for more information about the full range of these recognised qualifications.

Money

Starting salaries tend to be around £12,000 per year. You might receive bonuses or other financial benefits.

Career progress

More experienced customer advisers and team leaders can earn £14,000–£30,000+ per year. It is possible to train as a specialist customer adviser, a financial adviser or move into many other posts within the field of finance with the help of company training or recognised qualifications.

Financial Services Skills Council www.fssc.org.uk
IFS School of Finance www.ifslearning.ac.uk

Debt collector

Recovering money owed by businesses and individuals on behalf of clients

Debt collectors work for agencies on behalf of organisations needing to recover unpaid debts. These debts can be between businesses, or between businesses and consumers. Debtors are first contacted by letter or telephone, and if this does not work visits are made in person and finally solicitors are involved.

Pros and cons

○ If the job is office based, work tends to be standard hours.
○ If home visits are to be made, hours tend to include early mornings, late evenings and weekends.

- People can sometimes be confrontational.
- The work can pay well and there might be opportunities for promotion.

You

- Tactful, with good interpersonal skills.
- Confident and assertive when needed.
- Good understanding of the law.
- Awareness of personal safety issues.

Entry/learning

- No set qualifications are needed, but GCSEs in English and Maths are very useful.
- Training is mostly on the job.
- You can study part time to gain various qualifications from the Institute of Credit Management or City & Guilds.

Money

Starting salaries are around £14,000 per year. Some employers might have a bonus system.

Career progress

More experienced debt collectors can become team leaders or managers, earning £25,000–£35,000+ per year. Some people set up their own debt collection agencies, which might specialise in particular types of debt recovery such as personal or business debts.

Credit Management Training Ltd www.cmtltd.co.uk
Credit Services Association www.csa-uk.com

Trainee financial adviser

Consulting with clients about their financial goals, and advising them on financial issues and products

Financial advisers can be 'tied' and work for a particular financial institution, such as a bank, or they can be 'independent' and sell a range of products and services from different companies. They ask customers about their financial aims, and then advise on the best pension, mortgage or investment options to meet these requirements.

Pros and cons

- Some advisers work regular office hours, but others might need to work on Saturdays or evenings to meet the needs of their clients.
- There will be opportunities to specialise and get promotions.

- o   You might feel pressured to meet targets.
- o   You might have to travel a lot to meet clients.

You
- o   Smartly dressed and show a responsible and mature attitude.
- o   Good with numbers and analysing financial information.
- o   Good communication skills and sales skills.
- o   Keep up to date with changes in finance and the law.

Entry/learning
- o   Most employers ask for five GCSEs (grades A–C) or equivalent, plus two A levels or equivalent, although many entrants have a degree.
- o   It is possible to enter via an advanced apprenticeship.
- o   To become fully qualified as a financial adviser, trainees need to complete a Financial Planning Certificate from the Chartered Insurance Institute, a Certificate for Financial Advisers from the Institute of Financial Services, or another FSA-approved qualification. For more information, visit www.fssc.org.uk.
- o   By the end of 2012, all post-traineeship advisers will have to have an approved Level 4 qualification.

Money
Starting salaries are around £20,000 per year, with less for apprentices.

Career progress
You can specialise in different areas, such as pensions or mortgages, and possibly become a senior adviser, with wages from £30,000 to £120,000+ per year. Some people become self-employed.

Financial Services Skills Council www.fssc.org.uk
IFS School of Finance www.ifslearning.ac.uk

Human resources officer

Recruiting staff, arranging training and development, and looking after staff welfare matters

Human resources officers recruit and select staff, as well as help staff get the training and skills development that they need. They also negotiate with staff and trade unions on pay and conditions, and are involved with disciplinary procedures, complaints and redundancies.

Pros and cons
- o   You usually have a standard working week.
- o   The work can be rewarding, helping people to progress in their careers.
- o   You will have to deal with angry or upset staff occasionally.

You

- Enjoy working with others, and in a team.
- Tactful and discreet.
- Excellent communication skills.
- Understand employment laws.

Entry/learning

- There are no minimum entry requirements, but most officers now have degrees.
- Many employers ask for five GCSEs (grades A–C) and two A levels or equivalent.
- It is possible to enter this career via an apprenticeship.
- Once working, it is possible to gain qualifications from the Chartered Institute of Personnel and Development.

Money

Starting salaries are around £15,000–£22,000 per year for trainees.

Career progress

It is possible to become a senior officer or human resources manager, with experience and qualifications, earning £30,000–£60,000+ per year. You might have to move between companies to gain a promotion, especially if you're working for a small employer.

Chartered Institute of Personnel and Development www.cipd.co.uk

---

Personal assistant

Providing administrative support to senior members of staff

Personal assistants work for one or more senior staff members, usually managers or directors, helping them to be as organised and efficient as possible. This includes arranging appointments and other events, booking travel, and word processing documents such as letters and reports. The job also includes filing, greeting visitors and answering phone calls.

Pros and cons

- You usually have a standard working week, but you might need to put in overtime during busy periods.
- It can be a stepping stone to other jobs within an industry.
- The job can be varied and interesting.

You

- Reliable and very discreet.
- Well organised and able to work under pressure.

- o Excellent interpersonal skills.
- o Good standard of English and IT skills.

Entry/learning
- o There are often no set entry requirements, but having GCSEs in English and Maths is an advantage.
- o Some employers might ask for A levels or business qualifications.
- o Entry can also be via apprenticeships.
- o Most training is on the job, but you can also study part time for NVQs and City & Guilds qualifications.

Money
Starting salaries are around £18,000–£19,000 per year.

Career progress
You can become a team leader, start working for a more senior manager, or change business areas, earning £24,000–£42,000 per year. The general business knowledge gained from working in an industry can lead to work in other areas such as management, publicity or sales.

Council for Administration www.cfa.uk.com

Receptionist

Greeting visitors as they arrive at an organisation, and dealing with their requests efficiently

Receptionists welcome visitors, issue security passes or sign people in, and direct visitors to their meetings, or arrange for them to be collected by other staff. They might also deal with general enquiries and book taxis, answer phone calls, accept deliveries, keep the reception area tidy and provide drinks for people who are waiting.

Pros and cons
- o You usually have a standard working week, unless you're working in a hotel or some hospital departments.
- o It is a sociable job where you are meeting new people every day.
- o You might need to wear a uniform.

You
- o Friendly, helpful and welcoming.
- o Smartly dressed.
- o Well organised, practical and efficient.
- o Tactful, with good customer service skills.

Entry/learning

- o There are no set entry requirements, but some employers will ask for GCSEs or NVQs, and the new Diploma in Business, Administration and Finance might be relevant.
- o Work experience is very helpful.
- o Apprenticeships might be available.
- o Most training is on the job, but you can also study part time to gain NVQs/ SVQs in subjects such as reception, customer service or business and administration.

Money

Starting salaries are around £11,000–£12,000 per year.

Career progress

You can become a team leader or reception manager with experience, earning £18,000 to £24,000+ per year. Some people move into office work or other posts within an organisation, such as administrative assistant or personal assistant jobs.

Council for Administration Careers www.breakinto.biz

Interview

Laura, Receptionist,
age 21

'I wanted to work in one of the creative industries, so I signed up with some employment agencies that specialise in talent, fashion, design and architecture placements before I left school. Agencies like that have so many options that you can't find yourself, no matter how much you search online, and they knew some of the employers really well so they gave me interview tips for each job too, what to say, what to wear. I did temp jobs for a while then they found me a permanent job in this marketing agency and I've been here for nearly three years now. They wanted to check I had core GCSEs and was computer literate, but mostly they wanted to know if I had people skills and could work well under pressure, and about personal drive and qualities.

'We work from 8.30a.m. to 5.30p.m. here, which is quite sociable hours. I have a lot of different duties: meeting and greeting, being the public face of the company, making tea and coffee for visitors, setting up meeting rooms, photocopying, arranging and ordering stationery, ordering catering for meetings, and keeping the reception area clean and tidy and welcoming for clients because we need to create a calm and relaxing atmosphere. Work can be pressurised, you can get pulled in five directions at once and sometimes you get blamed for things that are not your fault. You need to stay composed and not shout back. I like meeting lots of different people and every day is different, and I get to know everyone in the company. I've asked around at work and people say there are some PA and admin assistant jobs coming up, so I'm going to apply for those because I'm ready to take on some new duties.'

Secretary Ⓐ

Providing administrative support for a team or a manager in an organisation

Secretaries organise meetings, coordinate team diaries, book meeting rooms and other venues, take minutes during meetings, answer telephones and type letters and reports. They might also make travel arrangements, create and maintain filing systems, and deal with post.

Pros and cons
- You usually have a standard working week, with occasional overtime during busy periods.
- The job gives you good working knowledge of the organisation you're in.
- The tasks can often be routine.
- Deadlines and workload can be stressful.

You
- Organised, efficient and able to prioritise.
- Excellent interpersonal skills.
- Confident with numbers and working with IT.
- Work well under pressure.

Entry/learning
- There are no set entry requirements but many posts ask for GCSEs or equivalent; the new Diploma in Business, Administration and Finance might be relevant.
- Good standard of English, shorthand or word processing skills, and work experience are all helpful.
- Some apprenticeships are available.
- You can also start as an office junior and work your way up.

Money
Salaries start at around £11,000–£13,000 per year.

Career progress

You can become a senior secretary or a team leader, earning £25,000–£40,000+ per year for some types of work. Some people become personal assistants to directors, or move into office management.

Council for Administration Careers www.breakinto.biz

Other jobs to consider

- Accounting clerk ⓐ
- Assistant registrar of births, deaths, marriages and civil partnerships
- Civil service administrative assistant/officer
- Estates officer's assistant
- Farm secretary
- Junior pensions administrator ⓐ
- Legal secretary ⓐ
- Medical secretary
- Paraplanner ⓐ
- Payroll clerk ⓐ
- Post Room assistant
- Switchboard operator/telephonist.

Family 2
Building and construction

About two million people currently work in building and construction in the UK. This job family covers a wide range of different jobs, including craft-based, sales-based and design-based work. Many people start their working lives in the craft-based jobs by applying for apprenticeships.

Many of these jobs require a good level of fitness and the ability to work well with your hands, and all of them require much attention to detail. It is also common to be working outside for part or all of the working day, so for many of these jobs it helps if you like being outdoors. Teamwork is very important, and so is being able to follow any health and safety guidelines that are given.

Employers might be large international construction firms, national estate agent chains, local councils, or small- or medium-sized businesses. Many people who work in building and construction set up their own business and work as contractors.

Jobs and contacts

Bricklayer A

Building and repairing walls using bricks, stones and mortar

Working outdoors on sites or indoors on internal walls, cutting bricks to shape and layering them up with mortar. The walls have to follow the building plans and be built to a safe standard. Bricklayers check that their work is straight and level by using measuring tools as they go along.

Pros and cons
- You usually have a standard working week, but some people might have early starts to make the best use of daylight hours.

- You will need to do heavy physical work, involving lots of standing, bending and lifting.
- You will work mostly outdoors, so it can be cold and rainy, dusty or muddy.

You

- Practical and enjoy manual work.
- Physically fit.
- Able to follow plans and check own work.
- A head for heights.

Entry/learning

- There are no set entry requirements, but GCSEs in Maths or Design and Technology can be useful, and so can vocational qualifications from school or college.
- Many people start working in this area through apprenticeships.
- NVQs/SVQs are available in Bricklaying at Levels 1–3.
- There are also BTEC First Diplomas and City & Guilds certificates.

Money

Trainees can earn £7,000–£13,000 per year, going up to around £17,000 with Level 2 NVQs.

Career progress

Experienced bricklayers can earn £25,000+ per year, with a chance to earn more as a supervisor. Most people eventually become self-employed and work as contractors on building sites, or renovating people's homes.

Construction Skills www.bconstructive.co.uk

Carpenter/joiner Ⓐ

Making, installing and repairing items made of wood

Carpenters work on wooden items, making floorboards, window frames, cupboards, doors, kitchen units and many other things. Sometimes they work with hand tools such as planes and chisels, and other times they work with power tools such as electric drills and sanders. Some work is indoors or in a workshop, and travel to outdoor sites might be required.

Pros and cons

- You usually have a standard working week.
- You will feel a sense of achievement when you see your finished work.
- You might need to wear protective clothing and a mask.
- The work involves lots of dust, often working outside.

You

o Practical, good at manual work and maths.
o Good attention to detail and able to follow plans.
o Understand health and safety issues.
o Physically fit.

Entry/learning

o There are no set entry requirements, but GCSEs in Maths and Design and Technology can be useful, as can vocational studies at school, and perhaps also the new Diploma in Construction and the Built Environment.
o Apprenticeships are available.
o You can also study part time while you're working to gain NVQs/SVQs at Levels 1–3, Institute of Carpenters awards or a range of woodwork-related City & Guilds certificates.
o You will need a Construction Skills Certificate Scheme card if you want to work on a construction site. See www.cscs.uk.com for details.

Money

Trainees earn around £9,500–£16,000 per year.

Career progress

With experience and training, some carpenters become supervisors, managers or tutors, earning £17,000–£40,000+ per year. Many become self-employed, and some specialise in the renovation and repair of old buildings or furniture.

Construction Skills www.bconstructive.co.uk
Institute of Carpenters www.instituteofcarpenters.com

Construction operative

Working as part of a team on building projects, making houses, roads, bridges and other structures

Work can vary, but might include mixing cement and plaster, digging trenches, operating construction equipment and driving vehicles. Operatives also help to lay foundations and drains, and put up safety signs and huts. Most work is outdoors in all weather conditions.

Pros and cons

o You usually have a standard working week, but some people will have an early start to make the most of daylight hours.
o You might have the opportunity to work overtime.
o The work is physically demanding, but seeing the results of your work can be very satisfying.
o You will often have to work in dirty or dusty conditions.

You

- o Practical, physically fit and good at manual work.
- o A head for heights or depths.
- o Aware of health and safety issues.
- o Trustworthy and flexible.

Entry/learning

- o There are no set entry requirements, but a GCSE in Maths or Design and Technology is useful, as are vocational studies.
- o Apprenticeships are a common route into this field of work.
- o Most training is on the job, but you might be sent on health and safety courses as well.
- o You need a Construction Skills Certificate Scheme card if you want to work on a construction site.

Money

Trainees can earn £9,000–£12,000 per year.

Career progress

Skilled construction operatives can earn £16,000–£20,000+ per year, and overtime and bonuses can increase earnings. Some people become specialists, supervisors, or self-employed.

Construction Skills www.bconstructive.co.uk

Electrician Ⓐ

Installing, testing and maintaining the wiring systems in buildings and mechanical equipment

Electricians work on wiring systems to make sure that they are safe and working correctly. They follow detailed wiring diagrams and plans, and have to work safely at all times. They might work on housing or commercial developments, with computer networks, manufacturing equipment and many other types of electrical system.

Pros and cons

- o You might have a standard working week or work in shifts or attend call-outs to meet the needs of customers.
- o It can be very satisfying to solve electrical problems.
- o The working conditions might be cramped and uncomfortable.
- o You will need to travel a lot to homes and businesses.

You

- o Good communication skills.
- o Careful, methodical and practical.

o Strong understanding of health and safety issues.
o Physically fit with normal colour vision.

Entry/learning

o Some employers ask for four GCSEs (grades A–C) including English, Maths and a science, others make you take an aptitude test.
o Most people start working in this field on apprenticeships or advanced apprenticeships.
o Fully qualified electricians usually have Level 3 qualifications or higher, including courses from City & Guilds, NVQs or BTEC National Certificates.

Money

Trainee electricians earn around £10,000 per year.

Career progress

Qualified electricians can earn £17,000–£25,000 per year, with the most experienced staff earning £35,000+. Some experienced electricians set up their own businesses, working on large or small building projects, or in homes and other buildings.

SummitSkills www.summitskills.org.uk
Joint Industry Board for the Electrical Contracting Industry
www.jib.org.uk

Estate agent

Selling or letting properties for clients, and earning commission

The work involves assessing and valuing properties, and advertising and marketing them to tenants or buyers. Estate agents also explain selling and rental procedures to buyers, show people around properties, and assist in negotiations between buyers and sellers.

Pros and cons

o Most estate agents work a 40-hour week, often with evenings and weekends included.
o Opportunities depend on the current state of the housing market.
o The work might involve meeting sales targets, which can be stressful.

You

o Excellent interpersonal and sales skills.
o Good with money and maths.
o Keep up to date with changes in housing laws and the housing market.
o Ideally you will have a driving licence.

Entry/learning

- There are no formal entry requirements, but GCSEs or the new Diploma in Construction and the Built Environment might be an advantage.
- Most estate agents start out as trainee negotiators and train on the job.
- Apprenticeships are available.
- It is possible to study part time for NVQs in the sale of residential property, awards from the National Association of Estate Agents, or qualifications from the Royal Institution of Chartered Surveyors.

Money

Starting salaries for trainees tend to be around £13,000–£14,000 basic pay per year, plus commission.

Career progress

With experience and extra responsibilities you could be earning £20,000–£40,000+ per year. It is possible to become a supervisor or an area manager in larger companies, although some people have to move to another business to gain a promotion.

Asset Skills www.assetskills.org
National Association of Estate Agents www.naea.co.uk

Glazier

Using specialist tools to cut glass and other window materials and fit them into place

Glaziers measure and cut glass accurately using hand tools, and fit it into frames or housings. They might also remove old or broken glass and create replacement panes. They work for glazing or construction companies, car repair firms, local authorities and shopfitting companies.

Pros and cons

- You might have standard working hours, or have call-outs at any time.
- You might be working indoors or outdoors, sometimes in bad weather.
- There is a lot of standing, carrying and heavy lifting involved.

You

- Good at measuring, and working with your hands.
- Physically fit enough to carry and lift heavy glass panes.
- A head for heights.
- Good customer service skills and a good team worker.

Entry/learning

- There are no set entry requirements, but GCSEs in English, Maths and Technology can be useful, as can vocational skills.

- Most glaziers enter the profession via an apprenticeship or traineeship.
- Most training is on the job.
- It is common to study part time for NVQs/SVQs in glass-related subjects.

Money
Starting salaries begin around £12,000–£14,000 per year.

Career progress
Qualified glaziers can earn £18,000–£35,000+ per year. Call-outs and overtime can increase wages. Most become self-employed and offer services to building firms or the public.

Glass Qualifications Authority www.glassqualificationsauthority.com

---

Painter and decorator

Protecting and improving the appearance of indoor and outdoor surfaces

Painters and decorators work on houses, other buildings, and large structures such as bridges. They work with wallpaper, paint, varnish, primer, plaster and other materials. They also prepare surfaces before decorating them by sanding, cleaning, repairing and sealing them as needed.

Pros and cons
- You usually have a standard working week, but some people might have to start early to make use of daylight hours.
- You might be working indoors or outdoors, sometimes at great heights.
- You might need to wear protective clothing, or a mask for paint fumes.
- There will be opportunities to be creative or artistic on some projects.

You
- Good customer service and listening skills.
- Understand health and safety issues.
- Physically fit with good manual skills.
- Able to work in a team.

Entry/learning
- There are no formal entry requirements, but some employers will ask for GCSEs or vocational subjects, and the new diplomas might be relevant.
- Many enter the profession through apprenticeship schemes.
- Trainees often work towards NVQs or City & Guilds certificates.
- If working on a construction site you must have a Construction Skills Certificate Scheme card, which requires passing a health and safety test.

Money
Starting salaries are £9,000–£15,000 per year.

Career progress
With training, and perhaps moving into a supervisory role, it is possible to earn £16,000–£25,000+ per year. It is common for painters and decorators to become self-employed.

Painting and Decorating Association
www.paintingdecoratingassociation.co.uk
Construction Skills Careers www.bconstructive.co.uk

Plasterer

Using plaster, cement or plasterboard in the construction, renovation or decoration of buildings

Solid plastering involves applying plaster or cement to internal or external walls, with a finishing coat to give a flat smooth surface. Plasterboard can also be used to create internal walls or partitions. Fibrous plastering is making or repairing decorative plaster mouldings, especially around ceilings. Employers include specialist firms, building contractors and local councils.

Pros and cons
o You usually have a standard working week, but with some overtime for certain jobs.
o You might be working indoors or outdoors, in all weathers.
o You might be working on ladders or scaffolding.
o Some plastering work can be creative or artistic.

You
o Good at working with your hands.
o A head for heights and physically fit.
o Understand health and safety issues.
o Able to work well in a team and be polite to customers.

Entry/learning
o No specific qualifications are needed, but GCSEs in Maths, English, and Design and Technology are useful.
o The main route into this profession is by apprenticeships.
o Most training is on the job, often with part-time study to gain NVQs.
o If working on a construction site you must have a Construction Skills Certificate Scheme card, which requires passing a health and safety test.

Money

Starting salaries are around £14,000 per year.

Career progress

With further qualifications, salaries can rise to £16,000 and go up to £35,000+. It is possible to eventually become a supervisor or manager, to qualify as a technician, or to become self-employed.

Construction Skills Careers www.bconstructive.co.uk

Plumber

Installing, maintaining and repairing heating, sanitation and water systems

Plumbers work with the pipework connected to sinks, baths, boilers, toilets, radiators, water heaters and so on. They fit and connect items, and carry out maintenance and repairs. Some of them also work on the water drainage systems on roofs of buildings.

Pros and cons

- You might have a standard working week, or provide a call-out service.
- You might be working indoors and outdoors, sometimes in uncomfortable conditions.
- The work usually involves travel to many locations.

You

- Practical and able to follow building plans.
- Good manual and measuring skills.
- Able to problem solve and work safely.
- Excellent customer service skills and a good team worker.

Entry/learning

- There are no set entry requirements, but it helps to have three or more GCSEs or equivalents.
- Many people enter this profession via apprenticeships.
- Training is mainly on the job, but it is common to study part time as well.
- You will need a Level 2 or 3 NVQ, or a Level 2 or 3 Diploma in Plumbing in order to have qualified operative status.

Money

First-year apprentices can earn around £7,500–£10,000.

Career progress

Qualified plumbers can earn £17,500–£30,000+ per year, with opportunities to move into technical, supervisory or management roles. Some people take extra qualifications and become 'Gas Safe registered' to work with gas central heating systems, which can increase their earnings.

Summit Skills www.summitskills.org.uk

Roofer

Building, repairing and replacing roofs of different types of building

Roofers make, maintain and repair roofs of homes and other buildings such as offices, factories and sports centres. They use specialist tools to work on flat or pitched (sloping) roofs, and work with a range of materials, from tiles and slates to felt and corrugated metal.

Pros and cons
- You usually have a standard working week, with extra work available at weekends.
- You will be working outdoors in all weathers.
- The work is very physical, with lots of carrying and bending.
- You will usually need to wear protective clothing.

You
- Physically fit, practical and enjoy working outdoors.
- A good head for heights.
- Understand health and safety issues.
- Good communication skills with customers and co-workers.

Entry/learning
- No specific qualifications are needed, but GCSEs in Maths, English, and Design and Technology are useful, as are vocational subjects and the new Diploma in Construction and the Built Environment.
- Most roofers start on a construction apprenticeship.
- Training is usually done on the job, plus part-time study to gain NVQs and City & Guilds certificates.
- Health and safety training is compulsory for building-site work.

Money

The minimum wage for trainees is around £13,000 per year.

Career progress

With more qualifications, experience and responsibilities, you could earn £15,000–£29,000+ per year. Some people start their own roofing company, and might specialise, for example, in working on flat roofs or on old structures that need repairing.

Construction Skills Careers www.bconstructive.co.uk
The Institute of Roofing www.instituteofroofing.org

Interview

Chris, Apprentice Roofer,
age 17

'I left school at 16 to work for my Dad, who's in the roofing trade. He has a small business, and to learn some more I started an apprenticeship this year with a bigger firm. Most people my age who want to be roofers have a relative in the business. We're doing real jobs here, with contracts and everything, you really have to put the effort in. You can't ignore all the health and safety either. I'm getting on OK now, and I'm doing the apprenticeship that lasts for about two years, and doing NVQs at the college in town. Afterwards I'm going to go back to working with my Dad for a while, and then might be learning some new procedures to help the business update and expand.'

Wastewater treatment plant operator

Monitoring and treating collected water to make it safe to use and drink, and returning it to customers

Operators run and maintain the equipment and monitoring devices at wastewater treatment plants. There are many different duties, which can include disinfecting septic tanks, filters and screens, taking water samples and running tests, and adding treatment substances to purify the water.

Pros and cons

- You might have a standard working week, or have to do shift work.
- You will need to wear protective clothing.
- The working conditions can be smelly and wet.
- You might get an opportunity to work with new technologies.

You
○ An interest in science, technology and the environment.
○ Methodical, organised and analytical.
○ Good communication skills and able to work in a team.
○ Committed to health and safety standards.

Entry/learning
○ There are no formal entry requirements, but some companies ask for at least four GCSEs (A*–C) or equivalent, including Maths, English and a science or technology subject, and some of the new diplomas might be relevant.
○ It is possible to gain entry to this work via a traineeship or apprenticeships.
○ Most training is on the job.
○ It is possible to study part time to gain water industry qualifications including Level 2 NVQs and City & Guilds certificates.

Money
Trainees start on around £11,000 per year.

Career progress
It is possible to progress to supervisory or training roles, or to become an inspector, superintendent or plant manager. Earnings can be £17,000–£25,000+ per year.

Energy and Utility Skills Ltd www.euskills.co.uk
Institute of Water www.instituteofwater.org.uk

Other jobs to consider

○ Asphalter/concreter

○ Carpet fitter/floor layer

○ Cavity wall insulation technician

○ Ceiling fixer

○ Clerk of works

○ Construction plant operator

○ Crane operator ❶

○ Damp proofer

○ Demolition operative

○ Electrical appliance servicer/installer ❶

○ Fence installer ❶

Getting a Job After School

- Housing officer's assistant **Ⓐ**
- Laminator
- Road worker/highways maintenance
- Scaffolder **Ⓐ**
- Shopfitter
- Town planning technician/support staff
- Wall/floor tiler
- Water/sewerage network operative.

Family 3
Catering and hospitality

....

The jobs in this family have a strong element of customer service, and workers provide people with food, drink and accommodation. Communication skills, friendliness and politeness, and the ability to work in a team are important elements of all these types of work. In many of these jobs, attention to hygiene and tidiness are needed as well.

Working hours tend to be non-standard, with extra hours being worked at lunchtimes, evenings and weekends. Some jobs require early starts or night shifts, and occasionally staying on the premises, especially if working for hotels or in private homes.

There are jobs at all levels in catering and hospitality, so workers often have opportunities to get promoted once they have some experience. This can be to posts such as head waiter/waitress, supervisor or manager. Some people, such as chefs and other caterers, for example, might also set up their own businesses.

Jobs and contacts

Cellar technician

Installing and maintaining the equipment that allows licensed premises to serve drinks that are fresh and at the right temperature

Work includes installing, troubleshooting and maintaining drinks delivery equipment. Planning and site inspection skills are needed, and it's essential to ensure equipment is connected correctly to a venue's water, electric and drainage systems. The job might also require you to train the staff to use the equipment.

Pros and cons
- You usually have a standard working week, but you might need to do 24-hour call-outs, or work at nights or weekends.

- o You will have to travel a lot from site to site.
- o You might be working in cramped, dark or wet conditions.

You
- o Able to work with computers and hand and power tools.
- o An interest in science and engineering.
- o Physically fit, practical, analytical and motivated.
- o Good communication skills.

Entry/learning
- o There are no formal entry requirements, but some employers might ask for GCSEs.
- o Technicians can study for the Cellar Service Installation and Maintenance award from the British Institute for Innkeeping.
- o NVQs, City & Guilds or BTEC awards are also available for part-time study.

Money
Starting salaries are from £12,000 to £18,000 per year.

Career progress
You can move into senior technician or management posts, earning £20,000–£35,000 per year. Some technicians also move into sales or other areas of the drinks industry.

British Institute for Innkeeping www.bii.org
People 1st www.people1st.co.uk

Chef

Preparing food in the kitchen of a restaurant or for a catering company

Chefs plan and prepare a variety of foods, depending on their seniority or employer. They might also train or coordinate other staff, keep surfaces clean, monitor stock levels and order ingredients from suppliers. Employers include restaurants, cafés, large workplaces, pubs, hospitals and fast-food concessions.

Pros and cons
- o This job gives a chance to be creative with food and drink.
- o Making customers happy can be rewarding.
- o The job is physically demanding, requiring you to stand for long periods in a hot environment.
- o The job involves long hours, especially evenings and weekends.

You

o Motivated and dedicated.

o Strong interest in food and drink.

o Good communication skills and able to work well in a team.

o Understand health and safety issues.

Entry/learning

o No academic qualifications are required.

o Apprenticeships are available.

o Most training is on the job.

o You can study for NVQs, foundation Higher National Certificates (HNCs) and a variety of specialist courses.

Money

Starting salaries are around £12,000 per year.

Career progress

You can work up to the level of sous chef, head chef or executive chef earning £25,000–£60,000+ per year. Some chefs open their own restaurants, do demonstrations of cookery on television, write for magazines or write their own cookbooks.

People 1ˢᵗ www.people1st.co.uk
Springboard UK http://springboarduk.net

Concierge

Working in the reception area of hotels and other organisations to welcome guests and help with luggage or enquiries

Concierges greet guests, make them feel welcome, and help them as much as possible with luggage, information and bookings. They often have to run errands and pass on messages, and might have extra duties such as organising cleaners or looking after pets.

Pros and cons

o You might have a standard working week or work in a rota or shift system.

o There is a wide range of responsibilities and tasks.

o There might be some carrying and heavy lifting to do.

You

o Enjoy meeting new people.

o Polite, friendly and helpful.

- Good organisational skills and practical.
- Responsible, reliable and discreet.

Entry/learning
- No formal qualifications are usually asked for, but previous experience of customer services or knowledge of a foreign language can be an advantage.
- Apprenticeships might be available.
- Training is mainly on the job.
- You can also work towards NVQs.

Money
Starting salaries are around £12,000 per year.

Career progress
You can become a head concierge or assistant general manager earning £20,000–£25,000 per year. If working for a large hotel chain, there might be opportunities to work abroad, or move into different office-based jobs.

People 1st www.people1st.co.uk
Springboard UK http://springboarduk.net

Housekeeper A

Keeping accommodation in a clean, welcoming and attractive state

Housekeepers manage a cleaning budget and staff such as room attendants. They keep bedrooms, meeting rooms and communal areas in a clean and welcoming state. Work can be in hotels, conference centres, the National Health Service (NHS), care homes and private residences.

Pros and cons
- The work often includes some unsocial hours, depending upon the type of employer.
- It can be hard to get promoted in some posts.
- There might be staff perks or discounts such as free or discounted accommodation or meals, or use of leisure facilities.

You
- Excellent time management and organisational skills.
- Able to manage and motivate staff.
- Good at explaining procedures and training people.
- Able to handle a budget.

Entry/learning

- Academic qualifications are not always required, but if you don't have any then you will probably have to take a more junior post and work your way up.
- Some jobs require A levels or Scottish Highers, or higher-level qualifications.
- It is possible to enter this career as an apprentice or trainee.
- Training mostly takes place on the job, but it is possible to study part time for NVQs.

Money

Starting salaries for trainees are around £12,000–£12,500 per year.

Career progress

You can become a senior housekeeper, and gain employment with larger establishments, with salaries from £14,500 to £40,000 per year. Experienced housekeepers might also become trainers or managers.

People 1st www.people1st.co.uk
Springboard UK http://springboarduk.net

Waiter/waitress

Taking food orders from customers, and bringing their meals and bills to them

Waiting staff prepare tables, greet customers and take their food and drink orders, explaining the menu if needed. They then serve the food and drinks, check that diners are happy with the food, and prepare the bills at the end of the meal. Most waiting staff also clear and clean the tables.

Pros and cons

- The working hours are mainly non-standard, with busier lunchtimes and evenings.
- Some customers might be difficult to deal with.
- It is physically hard work, involving much standing and carrying.

You

- Polite with good customer service and team-working skills.
- Clean and neat appearance.
- Good memory and able to handle cash.
- An awareness of health and hygiene issues.

Entry/learning
- No specific entry requirements are usually needed.
- Number skills and previous customer service experience are useful.
- Training is mostly on the job.
- You can study for NVQs or do silver service training.

Money
Starting salaries from around £7,500–£11,000 per year for trainees who work average shifts. Full-time trainee staff can earn £12,000–£14,500 per year.

Career progress
You can become a head waiter, silver service waiter or wine waiter/sommelier, earning £19,000–£25,000 per year. With more experience, it is possible to become a restaurant manager.

Institute of Hospitality www.instituteofhospitality.org
Springboard UK http://springboarduk.net

Interview

Emma, Waitress,
aged 19

'I've been working here (at this restaurant) at weekends for some spending money since I was 16, and when I left college last year the managers offered me more work, so now I'm working the lunch and dinner shifts from Wednesday to Sunday. It gets really busy on the weekends and sometimes the chef gets all stressed out and lippy during service if they're short-staffed. There's quite a high turnover here.

'I've been working here the longest out of the waiters, and I start a bit before them in the morning and help get the restaurant ready, make sure all the glassware and cutlery are laid out right, that sort of thing. Next thing I want to do is learn about silver service and maybe work at some summer or corporate events. I've heard the money's better, although you don't get tips most of the time. We put all our tips together here and share it out evenly, but I don't think that's fair, you have to work really hard to get tips most of the time and some people here don't try.'

Other jobs to consider

- Bar person **A**
- Cloakroom attendant
- Conference and banqueting assistant
- Door attendant/commissionaire
- Fast-food service assistant
- Hotel porter
- Hotel room cleaner/attendant
- Kitchen assistant/porter **A**
- School cook **A**
- Wine waiter
- Youth hostel worker **A**.

Family 4
Computers and IT

Nearly every organisation in this country needs to use computers and technology, so there are all kinds of different opportunities in this field which employs nearly a million people. Many of the jobs in computing and IT overlap with one another, but some are very technical, or are support roles, and others are more sales-led or creative.

The field is changing and expanding all the time, and workers need to keep up to date and be ready to learn new skills. Ability to work with computers is essential, and problem-solving skills are usually needed for all roles. Many of these jobs need customer service skills too.

Most of the work in this area tends to require Higher National Diplomas (HNDs), degrees or foundation degrees at entry level, but there are a few openings with relevant work experience or apprenticeships, and some school leavers are able to find support-level jobs such as helpdesk work. There are often opportunities to move into team leader or management roles, and to gain further qualifications.

Jobs and contacts

Software developer/programmer

Designing, developing, testing and updating computer software programs

The work involves using different computer programming languages to create codes from scratch, or to adapt existing software. It is usually part of a team project to build or improve a website or an interactive program. You will probably also be designing user-interfaces, running tests and getting rid of program bugs.

Pros and cons
- o You usually have a standard working week, but sometimes people need to work late nights or weekends to meet project deadlines.

o Some travelling might be required.
o It can be tough to get work in this sector without a degree.

You

o Logical, analytical and thorough.
o Good team worker.
o Excellent knowledge of IT and multimedia.
o Enjoy solving problems.

Entry/learning

o If you wish to enter this work without a degree or extensive work experience, you might be able to apply for a higher apprenticeship.
o You will need A levels or equivalent to apply for a higher apprenticeship.
o It can also be helpful to create a portfolio of previous software projects that you've worked on.
o Once working, most training is on the job but there are many professional development awards to study for too.

Money

Starting salaries are £19,000–£25,000 per year, with less for apprentices.

Career progress

You can become a senior programmer earning £28,000–£50,000+ per year, or become a project manager. Some people set up their own business and become software consultants.

e-skills UK www.e-skills.com
Institution of Analysts and Programmers www.iap.org.uk

Technical support person A+

Resolving software and hardware problems for computer users, either over the phone or in person

Work includes installing and upgrading computing equipment and software, helping users with software problems, and logging technical issues. When problems cannot be resolved by telephone or email, support includes visiting computer users in person and carrying out troubleshooting.

Pros and cons

o You might have a standard working week, or you might need to work in shifts to provide weekend and evening cover.
o There is often pressure to solve problems as quickly as possible.
o This work can be a stepping stone to other jobs in the IT industry.

You
- Able to work well under pressure.
- Practical and a good problem solver.
- Keep up to date with IT developments.
- Communicate and explain things well.

Entry/learning
- There is no set entry route into this type of work, but sound technical knowledge is always needed.
- Entry can be via apprenticeships and higher apprenticeships.
- You will need A levels or equivalent, such as the new 14–19 Diploma, to apply for a higher apprenticeship.
- Most training is on the job, but there are many further qualifications that can be gained while working.

Money
Starting salaries are around £13,500–£17,000 per year.

Career progress
With experience and qualifications, it's possible to become a supervisor, or a network manager or administrator, earning £18,000–£40,000+ per year.

British Computer Society www.bcs.org
e-skills UK www.e-skills.com

Website designer A+

Creating new or updated websites for clients, including how the website looks and how it works

This job involves the use of graphics, software and programming languages to build websites to a client's specifications. Each site has to have the right 'look' and be easy to use. Website designers lay out the webpages and add design elements, test website interaction and performance, test the website on different platforms and help to optimise site rankings on search engines.

Pros and cons
- Most web designers have standard working hours, although there might be some late night or weekend work too if there are project deadlines to meet.
- Some work is available on a part-time or freelance basis.
- The quality of your last piece of project work will strongly influence the choices of potential clients.

You

- Creative and technical.
- Good listening and communication skills.
- Able to work in a team.
- Able to work to deadlines.

Entry/learning

- The usual entry route is via a degree, foundation degree or HND.
- Higher apprenticeships in IT are available, which usually require A levels or equivalent qualifications.
- An excellent portfolio of previous work can be helpful.
- Training is often on the job, or people can be self-taught; there are various part-time study opportunities as well.

Money

Starting salaries are around £18,000–£20,000 per year.

Career progress

You can eventually become a senior designer or lead a design team, earning £30,000–£60,000+ per year. Many people become self-employed, and work for all kinds of different clients.

e-skills UK www.e-skills.com
British Interactive Multimedia Association www.bima.co.uk

Other jobs to consider

- Computer games tester **A**
- Computer hardware engineer **A**
- Computer helpdesk adviser **A+**
- Interactive media designer **A***
- Systems analyst **A+**.

Family 5

Design, arts and crafts

This job family currently employs over a quarter of a million people. Designers work on everything from cars and clothes to magazines, making everything useable and attractive. Artists use a range of materials to produce paintings, drawings, sculptures and other artwork. Craftspeople include silversmiths, goldsmiths and engravers.

Creativity, an eye for design, good drawing skills and manual dexterity are all needed by people who work in design, arts and crafts jobs. While some craftspeople use mainly traditional skills to make attractive items, most jobs in this sector are now dominated by computer-aided design (CAD) and many use modern manufacturing techniques.

Many workers learn on the job, but there are also apprenticeships and other forms of training available. With experience, many jobs can lead on to management positions or trainer roles. About a third of workers become self-employed and work with different clients, and expand their business as their career progresses.

Jobs and contacts

Jewellery designer

Designing, and usually making, different types of jewellery

Work involves researching designs and materials, and then creating detailed drawings and making original pieces of jewellery. The designs can be one-offs for specific clients, limited editions or mass-produced ranges. Various types of traditional or modern crafting methods might be used, such as silversmithing, enamelling, stone setting or engraving.

Pros and cons
- You might have a standard working week, or you might need to work longer hours to fulfil deadlines.

- Some jewellery designers work part time, and some become self-employed.
- It can be very satisfying to see people buying and wearing your designs.
- If you are self-employed it might be very hard to break into new markets when you're just starting out.

You

- Creative, with a strong eye for design and details.
- Up to date with fashion and jewellery trends.
- Able to produce fine work by hand.
- Business skills if you are thinking of being self-employed.

Entry/learning

- There are no set academic entry requirements, but GCSEs in Art and Design or Design and Technology can be helpful and so can a good portfolio of work.
- Craft skills tend to be more important than academic qualifications.
- Training posts and apprenticeships might be available.

Money

Salaries start at around £10,000 per year for trainees.

Career progress

More experienced jewellery designers can earn £16,000 –£50,000+ per year, depending on employer or sales figures. Some self-employed designers are able to grow their reputation and expand their businesses in certain markets such as high fashion or the high street.

British Jewellers' Association www.bja.org.uk
Crafts Council www.craftscouncil.org

Interview

Claire, Jewellery Designer,
age 19

'I went from enjoying a hobby to starting my own jewellery business this year. It makes a profit, but I have to do some extra office temping work as well sometimes to make ends meet. It launched this January, and I've learned you need to spend money to make money and see a business grow. I was doing a corporate job and I needed a creative outlet. I was a trainee travel agent, so I'd learned about some business skills.

'I saw an acrylic necklace I liked, and wanted to make my own, so I looked into it and downloaded some design software and learned how to use it to design the jewellery. I outsource the cutting and most of my designs use acrylic laser writing. Samples come back first from the cutting company and I check them before we go into production. A lot of self-promotion is needed to raise awareness – word of mouth, social networking, special events. I've booked stalls and sold at Camden and Spitalfields markets and I sell from my business website. I take regular feedback from customers, to see what they want to buy. There's nothing else that beats someone buying your work and saying how much they love it.'

Picture framer

Using specialist equipment to create attractive and protective frames and surrounds for paintings, photos, prints, medals and other objects

Picture framers first consult with customers about their framing needs and wishes, and then they create good quality frames in their shop or workshop. This involves a range of techniques and a variety of materials, including card, glass, wood and metal.

Pros and cons
- o You usually have a standard working week, but some shops open in the evenings and on weekends.
- o It is a chance to work with art and decoration.
- o Creating attractive and useful items can be very enjoyable.
- o You might have to deal with customers who might have complained about your work, or not liked it.

You
- o Good eye for design and some knowledge of art.
- o Precise and practical with your hands.
- o An understanding of the health and safety issues.
- o Good customer service skills and able to meet deadlines.

Entry/learning
- o No specific academic qualifications are needed, but GCSEs or other qualifications in art or design and technology can be useful, and so can practical experience in woodwork.
- o Most training is done on the job.
- o Once you're working, it's also possible to study part time on specialist training courses.
- o To work with high-value artwork, it's usually necessary to study art conservation.

Money
Starting salaries are around £11,000–£12,000 per year.

Career progress

Experienced framers can become managers or run specialist shops, earning £15,000–£25,000+ per year. Some people become self-employed and open their own business.

Creative and Cultural Skills www.ccskills.org.uk

Fine Art Trade Guild www.fineart.co.uk

Signwriter/signmaker Ⓐ

Designing and making two-dimensional (2D) and three-dimensional (3D) signs to attract attention or warn people

Signwriters/signmakers design and make indoor and outdoor signs, and sometimes also advertisements for the sides of buses or lorries. The materials used include plastic, paint, metal, wood and glass, and the techniques can involve traditional painting and lettering or more modern computer-aided designs. Work is usually carried out in a workshop or factory, but can take place outdoors or at a client's premises as well.

Pros and cons

- You usually have a standard working week, perhaps with some overtime on certain projects.
- There will be opportunities to be creative and practical.
- Working to deadlines can sometimes be stressful.
- The work can involve lots of standing and heavy lifting.

You

- Excellent design skills and creative.
- Able to use computer design software.
- Practical and good with your hands.
- Able to spell and have good communication skills.

Entry/learning

- There are no formal academic requirements, but GCSEs in Art, Design, English and Maths can be helpful.
- A portfolio of art or design work might also be helpful.
- Apprenticeships and trainee posts are available.
- Training is mainly on the job, and NVQs and other courses can be studied part time.

Money

For trainees, starting salaries are around £7,500–£12,000 per year.

Career progress

With experience or in management positions, earnings can be £17,000–£30,000+. Some signwriters become self-employed, and specialise in producing certain types of sign.

British Sign and Graphics Association www.bsga.co.uk
Creative and Cultural Skills www.ccskills.org.uk

Other jobs to consider

- Design assistant **A** **Q**
- Goldsmith/silversmith/engraver **A**
- Model maker **A**
- Musical instrument maker/repairer
- Staff photographer **A**
- Visual merchandiser/display designer **A**.

Family 6

Education and training

Education and training services help children and adults from all backgrounds to learn and develop. People who work in these jobs need to be organised and good time keepers and excellent communicators. They should also like lots of social contact, and be a supportive and patient type of person.

Some of the largest employers include schools, colleges, universities, play centres and nurseries. There are some workers who are self-employed and some others work for private clients.

Only a few types of education jobs are open to school leavers, and many of these are jobs related to childcare, or jobs supporting teachers or other school staff. Anyone working with children must undergo a criminal records check. Once you're working in this field, there are many opportunities to learn new skills, and to study for different qualifications.

Jobs and contacts

Nursery worker/nanny

Caring for babies and young children, and helping them develop and learn

Nursery workers and nannies feed, change, wash and dress babies, and encourage older children to develop social, number and language skills. They organise a schedule of meals, play, exercise and rest, and set rules for good behaviour. Work takes place at nurseries, some schools, and childcare centres for nursery workers, and nannies usually work in private homes.

Pros and cons
- The hours can be long and might involve shift and weekend work.
- Many people find working with children very rewarding.

- o The working day or week will vary.
- o The work often involves bending, lifting and playing.

You

- o Friendly, patient, tolerant and creative.
- o Understand the needs of babies and young children.
- o Aware of child safety and protection issues.
- o Responsible, organised and good team worker.

Entry/learning

- o There are no set entry requirements, but previous experience of childcare is helpful.
- o Some apprenticeships are available in children's care, learning and development.
- o You can study various childcare courses part time at college, including NVQs/ SVQs at different levels, and CACHE/BTEC diplomas.

Money

Starting salaries are £9,000–£11,500 per year.

Career prospects

You can become a team leader or manager. Senior posts can attract £23,000–£30,000+ per year. Some workers do further training to become nurses, social workers or teachers.

CACHE www.cache.org.uk
Children's Workforce Development Council www.cwdcouncil.org.uk

Interview

Ciara, Nursery Worker,
age 18

'I began working at my local nursery in 2009 as a volunteer and am now working full time. I really enjoy my job and am learning lots of new things with the children. I enjoy working with the younger children and particularly like working with the babies and toddlers. Recently I completed a food safety course and a paediatric first aid course, and right now I'm working towards my NVQ Level 2 and then hopefully moving on to do my Level 3.'

Playworker

Running a safe environment where children have freedom to play

Playworkers encourage children to learn through play, and create safe environments for this. They support and help activities such as drama, music, artwork, cooking and outdoor games. Work takes place in schools, play centres, youth clubs, hospitals, homes and other venues.

Pros and cons
- The hours can be irregular, seasonal, or involve evenings and weekends.
- The work is often great fun, in a creative and rewarding environment.
- Children can sometimes reveal sad or distressing information during play.

You
- Friendly, motivating, responsible and energetic.
- Good understanding of children's play needs.
- An awareness of child safety and protection issues.
- Good at building different relationships, and listening to children.

Entry/learning
- No official qualifications are needed to start working, but experience of working with children is an advantage.
- Most training is on the job, but you will probably be expected to work towards a recognised qualification as well.
- There are several qualifications in playwork, including NVQs, and CACHE and NCFE Level 2 certificates, plus diplomas in childcare and education.

Money
Starting salaries are around £11,000–£15,000 per year.

Career prospects
You can progress into management, training, or specialist areas such as hospital play, or set up your own play centre or events.

CACHE www.cache.org.uk

Teaching assistant/learning support assistant

Working with teachers to help pupils get the most out of a classroom learning experience

Teaching assistants/learning support assistants get rooms and equipment ready for lessons, listen to children read, and read to them. They also give one-to-one support and help children with special educational needs. More experienced assistants plan and deliver learning activities directed by a teacher, and assess and record children's progress. Work is mainly at mainstream or special schools at the secondary level.

Pros and cons
- You mostly work during regular school hours.
- It can be very rewarding helping children.
- The work can sometimes be hectic or challenging.

You
- Patient, helpful and calm.
- Enjoy working with children.
- Understand child safety and protection issues.
- Good at working with children who have special needs.

Entry/learning
- There are no set entry requirements but most assistants must be at least 18, and previous experience working with children is important.
- Most training is provided on the job and on short courses.
- Apprenticeships in Supporting Teaching and Learning in Schools are available.
- There are several different Level 2 pre-entry teaching assistant certificates to study, plus more advanced qualifications.

Money
Starting salaries range from £12,000 to £16,000 per year.

Career prospects
Senior or specialist staff can earn over £20,000 per year. Some teaching assistants do extra training to become teachers, or move into other jobs that involve working with children, such as care work.

CACHE www.cache.org.uk
Training and Development Agency for Schools
www.tda.gov.uk/leaders/supportstaff/cdf.aspx

Other jobs to consider

- Junior training development officer **A**
- Mentor **A**
- Private tutor (music)
- School/college administration assistant
- School lunchtime supervisor.

Family 7

Engineering, manufacturing and production

Many engineering and manufacturing jobs are quite specialised and need high level qualifications. However, there are still some options for school leavers, including lots of different apprenticeships. Most opportunities need workers who can concentrate for long periods of time and have good spatial awareness. You also need to be technical and methodical, and sometimes creative.

Employment figures

○ The manufacturing and production industry employs over two million people in the UK – around 10% of the working population of the country.

○ Engineering employs around 1.5 million workers.

Employees might be involved in research and design processes, or in production and manufacturing of a range of products, such as food products, electronics, cars and planes, furniture and chemicals. All jobs include essential health and safety training, and there are often opportunities to gain extra qualifications and advance to posts such as technician-level jobs or management positions.

Jobs and contacts

Assembler A

Putting parts together in a factory to create components or finished products

Assemblers usually work on a production line or at a bench in a factory or workshop. They take ready-made parts to produce completed products or electrical components. Work includes engineering projects, electrical circuit boards, domestic electrical equipment, cars, furniture, toys, convenience foods, and pharmaceutical products.

Pros and cons

- You might have a standard working week, or work in shifts.
- Factories are often noisy and busy.
- The work can be repetitive and monotonous.
- Many employers have clear structures for promotion, and some offer bonus schemes.

You

- Practical, quick and precise.
- Good attention to detail.
- Able to follow diagrams or instructions.
- Normal colour vision (for working with electrical products).

Entry/learning

- No set qualifications are required, but some employers might ask for GCSEs or equivalent; the new diplomas or vocational or practical studies might be useful.
- Apprenticeships might be available.
- Most training is on the job.
- It is possible to study part time for NVQs while working.

Money

Starting salaries are around £10,000–£12,000 per year.

Career progress

More experienced and skilled assemblers can earn from £12,000 to £20,000+ per year, perhaps with bonuses on top of this.

Semta www.semta.org.uk

Interview

Jack, Assembly Line Worker,
age 18

'The main jobs you can get in this part of town are in meat processing, at the sewage farm, or here where they make and pack medicines. There are lots of production lines here for different things, like indigestion tablets, and inhalers, they move you around between them. The factory is kept very clean, there are lots of rules, you even have to wear a special hair net on your chin if you have a beard. There's a really cheap canteen with subsidised food, a gym you can use for free whenever you like, staff outings and things.'

Baker **A**

Making a range of bread and pastry products

Bakers create many flour-based foods, and the work involves weighing and mixing, shaping, leaving the dough to rise, cooking, slicing, decorating and packaging. Some bakery operatives work mainly on one process, and others might carry out the whole range of activities. Employers include factories, supermarkets, bakery chains and small craft bakeries.

Pros and cons
- The working day usually starts early, and there might be shift work.
- The working environment is hot.
- It is very physical work with lots of standing.
- Work can have a lot of appeal for people who are passionate about food.

You
- Physically fit and a good team worker.
- Organised and able to meet deadlines.
- An interest in cookery and food.
- Follow hygiene regulations and instructions.

Entry/learning
- No specific qualifications are required, but English and basic maths skills are needed; food-related work experience is useful.
- Apprenticeships are available.
- There is a lot of on-the-job training.
- You can also take NVQs and other qualifications while working.

Money
Trainees earn around £13,000 per year.

Career progress
It is possible to take further qualifications and specialise in specific types of baking, or to become a supervisor or production manager, earning up to £35,000+ per year. Some people set up their own business, such as a craft or local bakery.

Improve www.improveltd.co.uk

CAD draughtsperson

Using CAD to create technical drawings and instructions to help others make structures, equipment or components

A CAD draughtsperson works from design drawings, a 3D model or a computer model of an overall product or section. They use CAD to complete technical drawings for components, structures, or pieces of equipment. They might be employed in industries such as construction, electronics, engineering, design, and telecommunications.

Pros and cons
- You usually have a standard working week, with occasional overtime.
- Most work is carried out in an office or design area.
- There is a shortage of skilled CAD draughtspeople, which might help your employment prospects.

You
- Excellent IT and technical drawing skills.
- Ability to solve problems.
- Patient, accurate and a good communicator.
- Awareness of construction or production methods.

Entry/learning
- No particular qualifications are needed for basic-level entry, but you are likely to be asked for at least four GCSEs (A–C) or equivalent, including Maths and a science, or Design and Technology.
- Apprenticeships and advanced apprenticeships are available, and some employers offer trainee technician posts.
- Training is mainly on the job.
- It is also possible to gain qualifications such as Level 3 NVQs, BTEC National Certificates or Diplomas, or City & Guilds certificates.

Money
Starting salaries are around £15,000–£18,000 per year.

Career progress
It is possible to become a senior draughtsperson or a supervisor, or to become a freelancer, earning £20,000–£40,000+ per year.

Enginuity Careers www.enginuity.org.uk

Electricity distribution worker

Installing and maintaining the machinery and equipment that transmits electricity from power stations to properties

Workers check, maintain and replace the overhead lines, masts and underground cables that connect electricity networks together. They also install, test and repair equipment in regional electricity substations.

Pros and cons
- You might have regular working hours, or work overtime or shifts.
- Working conditions can be unpleasant, rainy or oily.
- The work can be physically demanding, with lots of lifting, carrying and bending.
- There are good opportunities to progress in your career or diversify.

You
- Excellent attention to detail.
- Practical and good with your hands.
- Physically fit and have normal colour vision.
- Always follow health and safety procedures.

Entry/learning
- Most employers ask for at least four GCSEs (A–C) including English, Maths and a science or Design and Technology.
- The main route into this work is via an apprenticeship.
- There is usually a mixture of on-the-job training and college-based study.

Money
Starting salaries are around £9,000–£10,000 per year.

Career progress
With experience you can progress to a more senior, team supervisor or management position, earning £19,000–£30,000+ per year.

Energy & Utility Skills www.euskills.co.uk

Food-processing operative

Preparing and packaging a range of different food products

Operatives might work with foods in one of several areas, including washing, peeling or chopping, canning, cooking, freezing, drying or pasteurising. They might carry out tasks by hand or use a range of light or heavy machinery. Tasks also include packaging and labelling the foodstuffs.

Pros and cons
o You might work standard hours, or shifts that include nights or weekends.
o The work is often very physical, with lots of standing and lifting.
o You will usually need to wear special clothing such as overalls and hats.
o The work can be repetitive at times, but promotion prospects are good.

You
o Work well in a team and physically fit.
o Follow instructions and guidelines.
o Able to spot problems as they arise and respond quickly.
o Respect food hygiene rules and understand health and safety issues.

Entry/learning
o There are no formal entry requirements, but employers usually expect you to have reading and maths skills.
o Apprenticeships are available in some areas of work.
o Most training is on the job, including practical skills, food safety and general health and safety.
o You can study for Level 1–4 NVQs in Food and Drink Manufacturing Operations while you are working.

Money
Starting salaries are around £12,000 per year.

Career progress
You can progress to a specialised area of food production, or become a team leader, night shift leader, supervisor or manager, earning £15,000–£20,000+ per year. Overtime, shift work and bonuses can increase earnings.

Improve www.improveltd.co.uk

Furniture manufacturing operative

Constructing and finishing furniture by hand or using machinery

Furniture manufacturing operatives cut and shape individual parts and assemble them to make a piece of furniture. They then smooth, sand and polish or varnish the piece, and might also add handles or upholstery. Some operatives make flat-packed furniture.

Pros and cons

- o You might have a standard working week, or you might have to do shift work; overtime is common.
- o You usually work in a factory, wearing protective clothing.
- o Seeing your finished work can be very satisfying.
- o Some tasks might be repetitive and boring, or physically tiring.

You

- o Good at working with your hands and enjoy making things.
- o Normal eyesight and good hand–eye coordination.
- o Patient, careful and accurate.
- o An eye for design and shapes.

Entry/learning

- o Most employers do not ask for any qualifications, but some might ask for specific GCSEs or equivalent.
- o Apprenticeships and advanced apprenticeships are available.
- o Most training takes place on the job.
- o Once you're working, you can gain work-based qualifications such as City & Guilds certificates or one of several different NVQs.

Money

Starting salaries are around £12,000 per year.

Career progress

It is possible to become a team leader, supervisor or shift manager, or to specialise in areas such as furniture restoration or design. Earnings can be £15,000–£25,000 per year.

Proskills www.proskills.co.uk

Gas network engineer

Installing and maintaining the networks of pipes that supply gas to domestic and industrial customers

Gas network engineers lay, repair or renew gas pipe systems, which often involves digging holes in roads, gardens or pavements. They also connect mains gas supplies to customers' premises, and respond to emergency calls about possible gas escapes.

Pros and cons

- o There is usually a standard working week, plus a rota for covering weekends and emergency call-outs.
- o Work is mainly outdoors in all weathers and involves digging.

- Protective clothing and safety equipment must be used.
- You can be exposed to dangerous materials.

You

- Physically fit and able to work carefully with tools.
- Able to understand technical instructions, computer generated plans and blueprints.
- Strong understanding of health and safety issues.
- Work well in a team.

Entry/learning

- No formal qualifications are required to start as a trainee, but employers tend to ask for four GCSEs (A–C) including Maths and English, a science and a technical subject.
- Work experience in engineering or building work can be helpful, as can a clean driving licence.
- Apprenticeships and advanced apprenticeships are available.
- Once you're working, it is possible to study for Level 2–3 NVQs/SVQs, and later to apply for an HND or degree.

Money

New apprentices earn £10,000–£11,000 per year.

Career progress

With experience and qualifications it is possible to progress to technician, supervisory or management positions, earning £17,000–£30,000 per year. Employers tend to have a well-defined structure for promotions.

Energy & Utility Skills Careers www.euskills.co.uk/careers

Trainee gas service technician

Installing, maintaining and repairing gas systems and appliances in homes, businesses and industrial premises

Gas service technicians work with gas fires, cookers, central heating systems and industrial equipment, and search for and repair gas leaks. They use hand tools, specialist plumbing tools, and specialist instruments to complete and assess their work.

Pros and cons

- You usually have a standard working week, but there might also be a call-out rota.

- The work is mainly carried out on customers' premises, and occasionally outdoors.
- You might occasionally need to work in cramped conditions.
- You might be exposed to dangerous materials.

You
- Good practical skills and able to use tools and measuring devices.
- Physically fit with normal colour vision.
- Good customer service skills.
- Understand technical information and respect health and safety regulations.

Entry/learning
- School leavers start work as trainees or apprentices, and usually need four or more GCSEs (A–C) or equivalent.
- Qualified technicians are registered with the Gas Safe Register.
- Work experience is essential to meet the registration requirements, and can be gained during an apprenticeship or working for a registered business that provides extensive in-house training.
- You will also have to work towards an NVQ in Domestic Natural Gas Installation and Maintenance at Level 2 or 3.

Money
Trainees earn around £12,000 per year.

Career progress
After registration and with further experience it is possible to progress into supervisory or management roles, earning up to £40,000 per year, or to become self-employed.

British Gas Energy Academy www.britishgasacademy.co.uk
Energy & Utility Skills www.euskills.co.uk

Knitting/sewing machinist

Making a range of garments by hand or by machine

Knitting/sewing machinists create garments using hand sewing and knitting, and by using knitting and sewing machines. They might also finish garments with trims, zips, buttons and embroidery. Some workers create entire garments from start to finish, whereas others work at one specific stage of the production process.

Pros and cons
- You usually have a standard working week with some opportunities for overtime.
- The work tends to be in a factory, which can be noisy and busy.

- You will be working in a team and on your own initiative.
- There might be a chance to be creative and work in fashion.

You

- An eye for design, colour, shape and fashion.
- Good attention to detail.
- Manual skills for operating machinery and completing fiddly tasks.
- Able to work to deadlines and high standards.

Entry/learning

- There are no specific entry requirements, but sewing or knitwear ability is important.
- Apprenticeships are available, and applicants are likely to be asked for some GCSEs.
- Most training takes place on the job, and some employers even have their own training school.
- Once you're working, you can also study for a Level 2 NVQ.

Money

Starting salaries are around £10,000–£12,000 per year.

Career progress

With experience and qualifications it is possible to progress into senior, specialised or sample-making roles, earning £13,000–£19,000 per year. Some machinists eventually become clothing designers.

Skillset Careers www.skillset.org/careers
Can U Cut It? www.canucutit.co.uk

Locksmith

Selling, installing, maintaining and replacing locks, and cutting keys

Locksmiths sell and replace locks for houses, cars and businesses, and cut replacement keys. Some also run call-out services for people who have lost keys or had them stolen, helping them to get back into their homes or workplaces. Locksmith businesses sometimes offer other services, such as the installation and repair of security systems.

Pros and cons

- You often have regular daytime working hours, usually including Saturday.
- Some locksmiths offer a 24-hour call-out service.

- The work can be varied and interesting.
- You might occasionally have to deal with people who are distressed.

You
- Good customer service skills and ability to stay calm.
- Good at problem solving.
- Trustworthy and honest.
- Work well with your hands and with tools.

Entry/learning
- Some employers ask for GCSEs in English, Maths, and perhaps Design and Technology.
- Apprenticeships are available and so are trainee jobs.
- Training is mainly on the job.
- You can study for courses run by the Master Locksmiths Association (MLA), the British Locksmiths and Key Cutters Association (BLKA) and the UK Locksmiths Association, or take related NVQs.

Money
Trainees can earn £12,000–£13,000 per year.

Career progress
Experienced locksmiths can earn £15,000–£30,000 per year and many become self-employed. Being prepared to answer emergency call-outs can increase earnings, and so can training to install and maintain different kinds of security systems.

Master Locksmiths Association www.locksmiths.co.uk

Machinist A⁺

Using machinery to create engineered parts from metal or plastic

Machinists make parts for all kinds of products, including domestic appliances, car parts and aeroplane engines. They use a variety of power tools, such as cutters, presses, drills and grinders, and computer numerically controlled (CNC) machinery in their work.

Pros and cons
- Working hours tend to be fairly standard, Monday to Friday, perhaps with some early morning starts.
- Some large companies operate a shift system.
- Factories tend to be noisy, and the work is physically demanding.
- There is a shortage of machinists in engineering, which is good for your job prospects.

You

- Excellent hand–eye coordination and manual skills.
- Able to follow and interpret diagrams and instructions.
- Happy working in a team.
- Physically fit with good eyesight.

Entry/learning

- The most common entry route is via an advanced apprenticeship started between the ages of 16 and 18.
- Most employers ask for at least four GCSEs or equivalent, including Maths, English, a science and Design and Technology.
- Training is usually a mixture of on the job and time spent at college.
- You are encouraged to study towards a Level 3 NVQ in Engineering Production.

Money

Apprentices start on around £8,000 per year.

Career progress

With experience it is possible to become a senior machinist, a team leader or supervisor, earning £16,000–£26,000+ per year. With extra qualifications it is possible to move into other engineering-related roles.

Semta www.semta.org.uk

Motor vehicle technician

Servicing and repairing motor vehicles

Technicians identify technical problems and carry out servicing and repairs on cars, vans, lorries, motorcycles, buses and coaches. Some also provide a call-out service, which is where they travel to vehicles that have broken down, and fix them at the roadside or tow them back to a garage.

Pros and cons

- Usually there are regular working hours, but some employers ask for overtime or shift work.
- Call-out services usually have a rota for staff, and you might have to go out in the middle of the night.
- The work can be enjoyable for people who enjoy motor vehicles and solving practical problems.
- The work might have to be carried out in cramped, oily or damp conditions.

You
o Technical and mechanical knowledge of motor vehicles.
o Team worker with customer service skills.
o Good level of fitness and normal colour vision.
o Methodical, fast and practical worker.

Entry/learning
o Many employers ask for at least four GCSEs (A–C) or equivalent, including English, Maths and a science.
o Many people enter this profession as apprentices or trainees.
o Most training is on the job, but some large employers have teaching centres.
o You can study for a range of NVQs, City & Guilds and BTEC qualifications in vehicle maintenance and repair.

Money
Trainees earn from £7,500 to £11,000 per year.

Career progress
You can become an experienced technician, a supervisor, a manager or a trainer, earning £16,000–£23,000+ per year. Some people set up their own businesses, which can specialise in emergency call-outs or specific makes of vehicle.

GoSkills www.goskills.org

Railway fitter/electrician

Maintaining and servicing mechanical/electrical railway rolling stock and machinery

Mechanical fitters maintain and service traction and rolling stock, plant machinery, passenger coaches, customer lifts and hoisting equipment. Electrical fitters work on the electrical side of the traction and rolling stock, plant machinery and passenger coaches. People work in teams, reporting to a senior technician or engineer, mainly in depots, with some trackside visits.

Pros and cons
o Much of the work takes place at night, so tends to involve shifts.
o Protective clothing and safety procedures are essential.
o It can be satisfying to know that the work helps to keep British transport systems running smoothly.
o The work might have to be carried out outdoors, at height, or in cramped, uncomfortable conditions, and is often very physical.

You
- Practical team worker with good manual skills.
- Methodical and safety conscious and be able to solve problems.
- Able to follow instructions and technical diagrams.
- Physically fit and have normal colour vision.

Entry/learning
- Most employers ask for three to five GCSEs (A–C) or equivalent, including English, Maths, a science and Design and Technology.
- Many new entrants start as apprentices or trainees.
- You will also have to pass a medical, and perhaps an aptitude test, and ideally you need your own transportation.
- Training is mainly on the job or on short courses, and you can also study for NVQs in Rail Transport Engineering.

Money
Apprentices earn around £9,500–£13,000 per year.

Career progress
Once qualified, you can earn £14,000–£30,000 per year. There is a well-developed structure for promotion in the railway industry, and it is possible to progress to senior technician or management jobs with experience and further study.

GoSkills www.goskills.org

Tailor/dressmaker Ⓐ

Making and altering a range of made-to-measure clothing

Tailors make bespoke clothing such as suits, jackets and coats. Dressmakers make a wider range of clothing including daywear, special occasion wear and formalwear, and bridal gowns. Both kinds of worker meet with their clients to discuss their requirements and for fittings, create designs, cut patterns and fine-tune the fitting, and embellish the clothes in a variety of ways.

Pros and cons
- You have regular working hours, usually including Saturdays and perhaps some overtime.
- There might be opportunities to progress, diversify and work abroad.
- There is a chance to be creative on a daily basis.
- Working in fashion can be fast paced and exciting.

You

- Excellent sewing and design skills and eyesight.
- Moderately physically fit and able to stretch and bend.
- Attention to detail and be creative.
- An eye for colours, fabrics and flattering cuts.

Entry/learning

- No specific entry requirements, but some employers ask to see evidence of sewing skills or want GCSEs (A–E) in English, Maths or Art.
- Apprenticeships are available to train as a Savile Row tailor.
- Most training takes place on the job.
- Courses are also available, including different BTEC and ABC awards and NVQs.

Money

Starting salaries are around £10,000–£13,000 per year.

Career progress

You can become a senior tailor or dressmaker, a supervisor, or move into designing, earning £14,000–£40,000+ per year.

Can U Cut It? www.canucutit.co.uk

Welder

Using heat to join metal or plastic sections, pipes or plates together

Welding techniques all use heat to join metal or heavy duty plastics together, and can be classed as manual, semi-automatic or fully mechanised. Most work takes place in a factory or workshop, but there might be some travelling to on-site locations. Protective gear must be worn and safety instructions followed.

Pros and cons

- You might have a standard working week or follow a shift system.
- Seeing your finished work can be very rewarding.
- You will be operating machinery and other equipment that is potentially dangerous.
- There are many career opportunities in this work around the UK.

You

- Good hand–eye coordination and manual skills.
- Physically fit and have good eyesight.
- Able to follow health and safety guidelines diligently.
- Patient and able to concentrate for long periods.

Entry/learning
- There are no set entry requirements, but some employers ask for five GCSEs (A–C) including Maths, English and a science, and the new Diploma in Engineering might be relevant.
- Apprenticeships and advanced apprenticeships are common routes into this profession.
- You can also study for related NVQs or BTEC certificates and diplomas.

Money
Trainees start out on around £8,000 per year.

Career progress
It is possible to move into specialist areas such as underwater welding, or to become a supervisor, earning £22,000–£80,000 per year. Some people study further to become engineers.

The Welding Institute www.twi.co.uk

Other jobs to consider

- Abattoir operative
- Brewery worker **A**
- Ceramic maker/decorator **A**
- Clothing presser/packer
- Footwear manufacturing operative
- Marine craftsperson/boatbuilder **A**
- Mobile plant fitter **A**
- Oil drilling roustabout **⊗**
- Paper manufacturer **A**
- Pipefitter **A**
- Quarry worker
- Textile operative
- Toolmaker
- Vehicle fitter **A**.

Family 8

Environment, animals and plants

Over a million people work with the environment or animals and plants in Britain. If you are passionate about the environment or care about animal welfare there are several types of job that might interest you.

Much of the work in this sector takes place outdoors, often in the countryside. For some jobs, specialist training is needed, but for other jobs a worker's personality and attitude are more important. Physical fitness is essential for most of these jobs. Working hours tend to be flexible, and they are sometimes irregular because they might change with the seasons.

Employers are mainly small businesses, although for some jobs it is possible to work for national or international companies as well. With experience it is possible to go on to supervisory or management jobs, but people might need to move to a different employer to progress. Skilled workers might also have an opportunity to travel and work abroad.

Jobs and contacts

Animal care assistant

Providing day-to-day care for animals, looking after their feeding and general welfare

Assistants feed, clean and groom animals, clean their accommodation and bedding, and monitor them for signs of distress or illness. They might also work with customers, dealing with enquiries and keeping records. Employers include animal boarding and grooming businesses, local authorities and animal-breeding businesses.

Pros and cons
- The working week is non-standard, often involving shifts.
- Many people find caring for animals very rewarding.
- Some duties are repetitive and messy.
- The work can involve lots of hard physical work.

You

- Like being around animals and have a confident manner with them.
- Team worker with good customer service skills.
- Observant and able to work on your own initiative.
- Happy working outdoors with certain animals.

Entry/learning

- There are no set entry requirements, but some employers might ask for GCSEs or other qualifications.
- Previous experience with pets and other animals, volunteering or work experience can be an advantage.
- Apprenticeships might be available.
- Most training takes place on the job, and it's possible to study part time for NVQs and other qualifications.

Money

Starting salary can be the national minimum wage, which from October 2010 is: £3.64 an hour for workers aged 16–17, and £4.92 an hour for workers aged 18–20.

Career progress

It is possible to become a supervisor or manager, earning £14,000+ per year. Some people start their own business such as kennels, catteries, grooming services or pet care retail.

The Pet Care Trust www.petcare.org.uk
Lantra Careers www.afuturein.com

Arboricultural worker Ⓐ

Planting, pruning and looking after trees in parks, gardens and on roadsides

Arboricultural workers might take directions from landscapers, garden designers or park planners. They plant trees, prune shrubs and remove branches, and carry out surveys to look at tree growth, or pests and diseases. Work often involves using chainsaws and other tools, and ladders, ropes and other climbing equipment.

Pros and cons

- There are usually standard working hours, with more work during the summer.
- You might have to work weekends or do emergency call-outs.
- It is a truly outdoor job and physically very demanding.
- You will be working with potentially dangerous power tools.

You

- Good at handling trees and shrubs, organised and practical.
- Physically fit, good with heights and not allergic to tree pollen.
- Follow health and safety regulations.
- You also need to have good customer service skills and be able to communicate well.

Entry/learning

- Many entrants have degrees or HNCs/HNDs in arboriculture or horticultural subjects.
- Previous work experience is an advantage.
- Apprenticeships might be available.
- It is possible to take part-time courses while working to gain NVQs and other qualifications.

Money

Starting salaries are around £12,000–£16,000 per year.

Career progress

It is possible to move into more senior or management jobs, earning £18,000–£35,000 per year. Some people become self-employed – working in gardening, woodland management or 'tree surgery' businesses

The Arboricultural Association www.trees.org.uk
Lantra Careers www.afuturein.com

Interview

Matt, Arboricultural Worker,
age 18

'Before I started my apprenticeship I did work experience with a local tree surgeon and it was really nice to be outside, going to places you might not normally go to, like out on the Downs. Sometimes the work was a bit repetitive but there is something satisfying about seeing the work completed, looking at an altered tree or part of the landscape. It is quite hard work though and you have to like being outside. Jobs are hard to find if you don't have training, I started here a year ago on an apprenticeship and I have one more year to go. One day a fortnight I go to the local college.

'Some of the machinery is dangerous, and at work they didn't let me near chainsaws for the first six months, they said it was for the insurance, and we get so much safety training and supervision. Most of the work you do when you start out is like loading trucks, checking equipment, assisting climbers who are using ropes, and there's lots of cleaning up and raking. You need special tickets to work on some sites. Some times of the year are quieter than others, and the business takes on other work, including gardening, to keep going. In the future I might train to be a supervisor or go into sales, and I heard you can travel abroad too if you have the right skills.'

Countryside ranger Ⓐ

Encouraging visitors to enjoy the countryside, and monitoring and conserving the natural environment and wildlife

Rangers provide information to the public about the countryside, look after visitor centres and other public areas, and manage volunteers. They also patrol, monitor and conserve sites and the wildlife in them. They apply for funding, control budgets and run activities and projects.

Pros and cons
- The working hours are non-standard and you might have to work on some weekends, with more work in spring and summer.
- The work is all outdoors, and involves walking regardless of the season and weather.
- You often have to travel a lot between sites.
- There is much competition for the jobs.

You
- Enjoy nature, conservation and the outdoors.
- Physically fit and not allergic to tree or grass pollen.
- A driving licence.
- Confident speaker, writer and researcher.

Entry/learning
- There are no set entry qualifications, but some employers ask for HNDs or degrees.
- Previous voluntary or work experience is an advantage.
- Apprenticeships are available.
- Most training is on the job, or you can take short courses organised by the employer.

Money
Starting salaries are from around £10,000 to £18,000 per year.

Career progress
With experience and qualifications it is possible to become a senior ranger or countryside manager, or move into environmental conservation roles. Salaries are from £20,000 to £32,000+ per year.

Lantra Careers www.afuturein.com
Countryside Management Association
www.countrysidemanagement.org.uk

Farmhand Ⓐ

Planting, harvesting and storing crops, and/or taking general care of livestock

Farmhands have practical duties on farms that grow crops, rear livestock, or have both. Work with crops includes planting, tending, harvesting, storing and packaging. Work with animals includes rearing, feeding, handling, herding, milking, shearing and administering medication. General work includes repairing fences and buildings, and repairing machinery.

Pros and cons
- Working hours are non-standard, especially for animal care.
- You will be working outdoors in all kinds of weather, close to nature and usually in the countryside.
- The working conditions can be cold, wet or dirty.
- You might need to work with dangerous machinery or chemicals.

You
- Enjoy working outdoors and physically fit.
- An understanding of plants or animal welfare.
- Follow health and safety guidelines.
- Practical and have a driving licence.

Entry/learning
- There are no specific entry requirements for most jobs, but previous work experience is helpful.
- Apprenticeships are available.
- Most training is on the job.
- Short courses can be taken or you can study part time for NVQs and other qualifications.

Money
Starting salaries are around £7,500–£11,000 per year.

Career progress

Experienced farm workers can earn £12,000–£19,000 per year, going up to £20,000 if they become supervisors.

Lantra Careers www.afuturein.com
City & Guilds Land Based Services (formerly National Proficiency Training Council) www.nptc.org.uk

---

Fish farmer Ⓐ

Raising fish or shellfish on a fish farm, and preparing them for market

Fish farmers raise fish or shellfish, and feed and care for them until they reach a size where they can be sold. They then net the catch and prepare them for sale. The fish regularly need to be checked for pests and diseases, and protected from predators.

Pros and cons
- The working week is often non-standard, involving extra hours and weekends.
- Fish farms are often in remote, isolated areas, although coastlines and lakes can be beautiful surroundings.
- Market demand and prices can affect jobs, and diseases can wipe out stock.
- The work is mainly outdoors and can be wet and messy.

You
- Like working mainly outdoors.
- Physically fit and hard working.
- Understand animal welfare, and health and safety regulations.
- Observant and able to work alone.

Entry/learning
- There are no set qualifications needed for most entry-level jobs, but work experience is useful.
- Apprenticeships/Skillseekers might be available.
- Training is mostly on the job.
- To become a manager, extra qualifications are needed, such as a BTEC diploma, NVQs/SVQs or a degree.

Money
New employees can earn £10,000–£13,000 per year.

Career progress
With experience it is possible to earn £12,000–£20,000 per year, with managers earning up to £45,000.

Institute of Fisheries Management www.ifm.org.uk
Lantra Careers www.afuturein.com

Gardener Ⓐ

Growing and caring for plants in gardens, parks, grounds and plant nurseries

Gardeners sow seeds, plant seedlings, weed, deal with pests and diseases, and clear spaces for plants to grow well. The work also involves digging and preparing soil, and caring for lawns, hedges, shrubs, flower beds and borders. Employers include businesses, local councils, the National Trust and nurseries.

Pros and cons
- You might have a standard working week with early starts in the summer, or perhaps working at weekends.
- This is physical work, carried out outdoors in all kinds of weather.
- You will get an opportunity to be creative with design, and nurture plants.

You
- Physically fit and good with your hands.
- Understand the needs of different plants and be ready to learn.
- Good communication and customer service skills.
- Aware of health and safety issues.

Entry/learning
- There are no set entry requirements for most jobs, but voluntary work or gardening experience might be useful.
- Apprenticeships and traineeships might be available.
- Most training is on the job.
- There are many opportunities for further learning including certificates, diplomas, foundation and honours degrees in horticulture.

Money
Starting salaries are around £10,000–£12,000 per year.

Career progress
Gardeners can become team leaders or managers, or become self-employed, earning up to £20,000+ per year. Some specialise in small garden design, estate work or landscaping.

Lantra Careers www.afuturein.com
Horticulture Careers www.growcareers.info

Groom/stable hand Ⓐ

Being responsible for the daily feeding and welfare needs of horses

The work involves feeding, grooming, walking and mucking out horses, and cleaning their saddles and bridles. Grooms might also be responsible for keeping yards and fields clean and tidy. Employers include riding schools and trekking centres, police and army stables, horse hospitals and breeders, and racing stables.

Pros and cons
- The working week is non-standard, includes weekends and possibly work at night if a horse is unwell.
- Stables might sometimes be in remote locations, but can include beautiful countryside.
- Working with horses can be very rewarding for animal lovers.
- The work can be tiring, smelly and dirty, and horses can kick and bite when stressed or handled badly.

You
- Love horses and the outdoors.
- Physically fit and have lots of energy.
- Understand the needs of horses, and health and safety issues.
- Good team worker.

Entry/learning
- There are often no set entry requirements, but GCSEs, diplomas, horse riding ability and previous voluntary or work experience can all be helpful.
- Apprenticeships might be available.
- Most training is on the job.
- Further qualifications are possible, including NVQs, diplomas, and the British Horse Society exams.

Money
Starting salaries are often the national minimum wage, which, from October 2010, is £3.64 an hour for workers aged 16–17, and £4.92 an hour for workers aged 18–20.

Career progress
More experienced grooms can earn £11,000–£16,000 per year, and head grooms can earn around £20,000 per year. Some grooms move into management roles at racing stables, riding schools or other businesses.

British Grooms Association www.britishgrooms.org.uk
Lantra Careers www.afuturein.com

RSPCA welfare officer

Working for the Royal Society for the Prevention of Cruelty to Animals (RSPCA), investigating complaints and rescuing animals

Officers investigate complaints of animal cruelty, respond to emergency and wildlife call-outs, give owners advice or warnings, and rescue many different animals. They also make detailed reports, and take part in the prosecution of people accused of animal cruelty.

Pros and cons
o   The working hours are non-standard, and you might have to work in shifts and respond to emergency call-outs.
o   Rescuing mistreated or injured animals can be very satisfying.
o   Some people are abusive, and some situations can be dangerous.
o   There is much competition for these jobs.
o   The RSPCA has a well-defined career structure.

You
o   Calm, empathetic towards and confident with animals.
o   Excellent interpersonal skills.
o   Respect for laws, health and safety, and animal welfare.
o   Observant and physically fit.

Entry/learning
o   At least five GCSEs (A*–C) or equivalent are required, and you must be over 18 years old.
o   Previous voluntary or work experience with animals is needed, as is a full driving licence, physical fitness and ability to swim. You should not have a history of previous convictions.
o   RSPCA training lasts several months.
o   Once you're trained it is possible to study part time for further qualifications.

Money
Starting salaries are £16,000–£19,000 per year.

Career progress
With further training, and perhaps leadership experience, it is possible to earn £20,000–£30,000 per year.

RSPCA www.rspca.org.uk

Veterinary nurse Ⓐ

Assisting vets by caring for and helping to treat sick or injured animals

Helping vets by assisting during examinations and operations, providing advice to owners, collecting samples for diagnosis, giving medication and carrying out simple treatments. Nurses might also work in reception, or give day-to-day care to recovering animals.

Pros and cons
- You might have a standard working week, or might have to do emergency cover or weekend work.
- The work can be varied and interesting.
- Working with animals can be rewarding.
- When animals die or are put down, it can be distressing.

You
- Love working with animals.
- Organised and calm.
- Have previous voluntary or work experience with animals.
- Good interpersonal skills and ability to work in a team.
- Not squeamish.

Entry/learning
- To become a veterinary nurse you must follow a training scheme recognised by the Royal College of Veterinary Surgeons.
- One of these approved training schemes is available as an apprenticeship.
- The minimum entry requirements are five GCSEs (A*–C) or equivalent, including English, Maths and a science; entrants must be 17 years old or over.
- Once you've qualified there are further opportunities for study.

Money
Starting salaries are £10,500–£12,000 per year.

Career progress
More senior nurses or supervisors can earn up to £25,000 per year. To gain promotion it is often necessary to move between organisations.

British Veterinary Nursing Association www.bvna.org.uk
Royal College of Veterinary Surgeons www.rcvs.org.uk

Water bailiff

Maintaining lakes and rivers and everything that lives in them, and preventing poaching and other lawbreaking activities

Water bailiffs look after lakes, rivers and other waterways, caring for the fish that live in them and protecting the wildlife and ecosystem. They have to deal with ecological problems such as pollution and fish diseases, and also with people who are breaking the law (such as fishing without a permit or disturbing the peace). They have powers of search and arrest similar to those of police officers.

Pros and cons
- The working hours can include night shifts and weekends.
- You might have to confront and apprehend law breakers.
- You might experience long periods of time spent working alone.
- You will be working in the outdoors in all weather conditions, often in remote areas.

You
- Understand environmental threats facing waterways.
- Ready to learn about related ecosystems, fish biology, and laws.
- Good interpersonal skills and polite and friendly.
- Physically fit and enjoy working outdoors.

Entry/learning
- There are no set entry requirements for most work in this area.
- Previous work or voluntary experience is very useful, especially to do with angling, farm work or similar.
- You might be asked to have a medical or fitness test.
- Training is mainly on the job.

Money
Starting salaries are around £14,000 per year.

Career progress
It is possible to progress to team leader or manager, earning up to £29,000 per year. Some people move into related areas of work, such as fish farming or gamekeeping.

The Environment Agency www.environment-agency.gov.uk
Lantra Careers www.afuturein.com

Other jobs to consider

- Dog groomer
- Fisherman/woman **A**
- Forestry worker
- Gamekeeper **A**
- Garden centre worker **A**
- Groundsperson/greenkeeper **A**
- Horticulture worker **A**
- Kennel worker
- Landscaper **A**
- Livestock production worker **A**
- Parks officer.

Family 9
Healthcare

About 1.7 million people are employed in healthcare jobs in the UK. Healthcare jobs can be found in hospitals and clinics, daycare centres and residential homes, GP surgeries, laboratories, pharmacies, opticians and dental practices. The largest employer is the National Health Service (NHS), but work can also be found with local councils, the armed forces and private businesses.

Jobs tend to cover the diagnosis, treatment and prevention of illnesses, research into diseases and medicines, health education, and general care of those who are unwell. Support staff are also needed to keep buildings clean and hygienic, and to assist patients and other workers.

Some work follows standard office hours, but shift work and part-time work tend to be more common. Excellent communication skills and the ability to work well in a team are very important in all of these jobs. It is possible to progress into management roles with experience, and organisations such as the NHS and the armed forces have clear career structures. For some promotions, vocational or academic qualifications are needed.

Jobs and contacts

Critical care scientist

Maintaining and operating life support and patient-monitoring equipment in intensive care units

Critical care scientists set up, monitor, maintain and repair the specialist equipment and machinery used for critical care patients. This includes electrocardiograms (ECGs), ventilation devices, and fluid and drug infusion devices. The main employer is the NHS, but there are some opportunities in private hospitals.

Pros and cons
- Working on a life-saving team can be very rewarding.
- You might need to work in shifts, or work long hours.
- Patients and relatives are often under intense stress and skilful communication might be required.
- The work involves a lot of lifting, standing and carrying.

You
- Calm, able to concentrate and work fast under pressure.
- A mature attitude and good communication skills.
- Work effectively as part of a team.
- Good understanding of technology and health and safety issues.

Entry/learning
- There are no formal entry requirements for some jobs, but many employers ask for at least four GCSEs/S grades (A–C/1–3), A levels or degrees.
- Most training is on the job.
- Apprenticeships are available.
- You'll usually be expected to study part time for qualifications such as BTEC certificates or NVQs/SVQs.

Money
Trainees can earn up to £17,700 per year.

Career progress
Possible to train in specialist areas, or become a manager, trainer or head of department. Wages are from £25,800 to £37,000+ per year.

NHS Careers www.nhscareers.nhs.uk
Skills for Health www.skillsforhealth.org.uk

(Apprentice) dental nurse

Helping dentists to carry out clinical treatment and patient care

Dental nurses prepare the dental surgery for patients, have all instruments to hand and sterilised, use suction devices in mouths, and give patients advice and instructions. Employers can be NHS or private dental surgeries, or hospitals.

Pros and cons
- You usually have a standard working week, but some weekend or evening work might be needed.
- Usually the dental clinic is a pleasant and clean working environment.

o At the time of writing, there is a shortage of dental nurses in the UK.
o You will need to wear protective clothing and a uniform.

You
o Good team worker and like helping people.
o Excellent eyesight and manual dexterity skills.
o Organised and be able to pay attention to detail.
o Friendly and reassuring.

Entry/learning
o You cannot gain work as a full-time dental nurse as a school leaver – recognised dental nurse qualifications are needed first.
o You can begin work as a school leaver, usually without any academic qualifications, if you are accepted onto an apprenticeship scheme.
o Then you must study for a qualification recognised by the General Dental Council (GDC).

Money
Salaries start at around £15,000 per year.

Career progress
With extra training, dental nurses can become dental nurse tutors or train as dental hygienists, dental therapists or nurse specialists, with salaries from £17,000 to £33,000+ per year.

British Association of Dental Nurses www.badn.org.uk
General Dental Council www.gdc-uk.org

Healthcare assistant

Working under the supervision of nurses and other health professionals to take care of patients

There are many different, regular tasks that are required for hospital patients, including making sure they are generally comfortable. Other tasks are helping patients to wash, bathe, dress, eat, move around and go to the toilet. This work is mainly carried out in hospitals, care homes, hospices and patients' homes.

Pros and cons
o You usually work on a shift or rota system, including nights and weekends.
o It is physically demanding, with carrying and lifting involved.
o Stressed patients or relatives might sometimes be challenging.
o This work is essential to the running of healthcare workplaces, and helping patients can be rewarding.

You

- Work well in a team and get on with different types of people.
- Caring, a good listener and observant.
- Good understanding of hygiene and health and safety issues.
- Able to cope with unpleasant tasks.

Entry/learning

- No set academic qualifications are needed, but work experience or voluntary work can be an advantage.
- Apprenticeships are available.
- Training is mainly on the job, but there might also be opportunities to study for NVQs/SVQs.

Money

Salaries start at around £13,000 per year.

Career progress

Experienced staff might earn £18,000+ per year. Many healthcare assistants study to become nurses or move into staff management roles.

NHS Careers www.nhscareers.nhs.uk
Skills for Health www.skillsforhealth.org.uk

Pharmacy technician

Working under the supervision of a pharmacist, preparing, supplying and dispensing medicines and other prescribed medical products

Technicians prepare, label and dispense medicines and other medical supplies, and advise patients about correct usage. They are also responsible for monitoring stocks and checking expiry dates. Work is in hospitals and outpatients' clinics, high-street pharmacies, pharmacy sections of supermarkets and in pharmacies attached to doctors' surgeries or health clinics.

Pros and cons

- You might have a standard working week, or you might have to work shifts, late evenings or weekends.
- It can be rewarding to work with different patients.
- You might be on your feet most of the day.

You

- Ability in science and maths.
- Attention to detail, accurate and keep good records.

o Understand health and safety, and confidentiality, issues.
o Work well in a team and good at explaining things.

Entry/learning
o There are no specific entry requirements, but many employers ask for five GCSEs/S grades (A–C/1–3), including English, Maths and at least one science.
o Apprenticeships are available, and you will probably be asked for four GCSEs/S grades (A–C/1–3), including English, Maths and one science.
o Work experience is an advantage.

Money
Starting salaries are around £17,000 per year.

Career progress
You can become a supervisor with experience, or move into sales and become a retail manager, earning £20,500–£39,000 per year.

The Association of Pharmacy Technicians UK www.aptuk.org
NHS Careers www.nhscareers.nhs.uk

Phlebotomist

Collecting blood samples from patients and sending them to a laboratory

Phlebotomists take blood from people as painlessly as possible, label the blood samples and then send them to a laboratory to be analysed within a set time frame. They mainly work in hospitals and clinics, but sometimes have to visit patients in their homes.

Pros and cons
o You might have a standard working week, or need to work shifts or in the evenings or at weekends.
o You often work with patients who are afraid, or have trouble communicating, and helping them can be rewarding.
o The work involves handling blood products that might be infectious.
o You will need to wear a uniform.

You
o Calm, reassuring and practical, and able to communicate well.
o Good working with your hands.
o Excellent understanding of health and safety issues.
o Not squeamish about blood or needles.

Entry/learning
o Usually there are no set entry requirements, but four GCSEs/S grades (A–C/1–3), including English, Maths and one science might help you get more advanced work.
o Most training is on the job, after which you might be awarded a certificate of competence.
o You might be able to work part time towards Level 2 SVQs/NVQs/City & Guilds certificate.

Money
Salaries start at around £13,000 per year.

Career progress
With experience and training you can become a senior phlebotomist, or a supervisor or manager, earning £17,000–£33,000 per year.

NHS Careers www.nhscareers.nhs.uk
National Association of Phlebotomists www.phlebotomy.org

Other jobs to consider

o Health records clerk

o Hospital porter

o Sterile services technician ⊗ Ⓐ

o Laboratory technician/assistant Ⓐ (see p. 176).

Family 10
Languages, information and culture

Around 100,000 people work in British libraries and the cultural industries. Jobs in this sector are about organising and providing information, understanding and interpreting history, using languages or researching different cultures. Most of the opportunities in this category require a degree or similar qualification, or previous experience, but there are some apprenticeships and trainee posts available.

Weekend work and part-time work are both common, but anti-social hours, such as night shifts, are rare. Much of the work available to school leavers has an element of customer service included, so interpersonal skills are important. IT skills, attention to detail, and the ability to be organised are big advantages too.

Not all of the jobs in this sector have clear career paths, and workers might need to gain extra qualifications to get promotions. Fortunately, employers often give in-house training or encourage employees to study for continuing professional development.

Jobs and contacts

Library assistant Ⓐ

Helping with the day-to-day running of a library, including customer service

Work includes organising and re-shelving books and other materials, checking items in and out, collecting fines and helping library users with their enquiries. Library and information employers might be public services, government departments, hospitals, schools, universities and businesses.

Pros and cons
- You usually have a standard working week or work part time.
- Helping people can be very satisfying.

- o The workplace can often be very busy.
- o You can be on your feet most of the day.

You
- o Work well in a team.
- o Like helping people and have good interpersonal skills.
- o Organised and methodical.
- o Good IT skills.

Entry/learning
- o You will need at least five GCSEs/S grades (A*–C), and some jobs need A levels or degrees.
- o Apprenticeships might be available.
- o You can also study for qualifications while working, including City & Guilds Progression Awards, NVQs and diplomas, and CILIP or ASLIB courses.
- o Senior library assistants sometimes study to become library managers or librarians by doing CILIP courses.

Money
Starting salaries are £15,000–£16,000 per year.

Career progress
Library assistants can take on more responsibilities and start working for larger organisations, progressing into more senior posts. If they qualify as librarians there are other opportunities for promotion.

Chartered Institute of Library and Information Professionals (CILIP)
www.cilip.org.uk
The Association for Information Management (ASLIB) www.aslib.com

---

Museum/art gallery technician

Handling and helping to display museum artefacts or pieces of art

Technicians prepare gallery and museum spaces to hold exhibitions and displays. Work can include installing lighting, carpentry or artistic techniques, and cleaning, handling and storing the exhibits. Some technicians might also be expected to have security or visitor services roles.

Pros and cons
- o You usually have a standard working week, but with some extra hours on an irregular basis.

o You might get a chance to work with interesting, beautiful or historical objects.
o The work involves a lot of standing, carrying and heavy lifting.

You
o Creative and practical.
o Understand building security and maintenance issues.
o Careful, methodical, and able to pay attention to detail.
o Able to work unsupervised or in a team.

Entry/learning
o No formal qualifications are required, but previous work experience can help.
o Some employers ask for five GCSEs/S grades (A*–C), whereas others might ask for a degree in a relevant subject.
o Apprenticeships in cultural and heritage venue operations might be available.
o You can study for a Level 2 NVQ/SVQ in Heritage Care and Visitor Services, or a Level 3 NVQ/SVQ in Cultural Heritage Operations while working.

Money
Starting salaries are £13,000–£14,500 per year.

Career progress
You can eventually become a senior or head technician with a salary from £15,000 to £31,000 per year. With extra qualifications, some people move into archiving, assistant curator or conservation technician roles.

Museums Association www.museumsassociation.org
Institute of Conservation www.icon.org.uk

Museum/art gallery visitor services assistant

Working with museum or art gallery visitors to provide information and other customer services

Assistants welcome visitors, work on ticket or information desks, and answer questions about the exhibits. They might also be asked to watch over the security of exhibitions and displays, set up and dismantle exhibitions, work in the employer's shop, or give guided tours.

Pros and cons
o You might have to work at weekends, in the evenings and on bank holidays.
o You can spend a lot of time standing or walking.
o It's very enjoyable if you like art or history.
o There might be some lifting and carrying to do.

You

- o Good memory and attention to detail – to help keep up to date with what's in the gallery or museum.
- o Patient, helpful and friendly.
- o Good team worker.
- o Understand workplace safety and security.

Entry/learning

- o No formal qualifications are needed, but work experience or a good general standard of education are very helpful.
- o Some employers ask for five GCSEs/S grades (A* to C), and others might ask for A levels or Highers, or a degree in a relevant subject.
- o Creative apprenticeships might be available.
- o You can gain a Level 2 NVQ/SVQ in Heritage Care and Visitor Services, or a Level 3 NVQ/SVQ in Cultural Heritage Operations while you work.

Money

Starting salaries are from £11,000 to £15,000 per year.

Career progress

You can progress to team leader or services manager with a salary of £15,000–£19,000+ per year, or move into technician, marketing or education roles within the industry.

Museums Association www.museumsassociation.org

Family 11

Legal and political services

Legal services can be office-based or revolve around the courts, but jobs often require degrees or specialist qualifications. Most employees have standard working hours, but in reality many end up working extra hours during evenings or at weekends. People who work in politics can have irregular working hours, and much travel might be needed.

Many jobs in legal or political services without specific entry qualifications require previous work or life experience, and few are open to school leavers. However, it is possible to find some assistant and support-level jobs and traineeships, and to study part time for qualifications while working. A high standard of written and verbal communication skills is needed to do well in these jobs.

Change occurs on a regular basis in law and politics, so people in these fields need to keep up to date with the news, and be prepared to study for continuous professional development.

Jobs and contacts

Court administrative assistant

Making sure a court runs smoothly by booking dates, times and courtrooms, and making sure everyone has the right paperwork and knows where to go

Assistants help the court administrative officer to organise papers and information for court hearings, and prepare bookings and timetables. They might also help to carry out court orders after court hearings, including collecting fines. Time is mostly spent in courtrooms and court offices.

Pros and cons
- You usually have a standard working week, but there are occasional opportunities for overtime or part-time work.

- O You might have to travel between courts on different sites.
- O You sometimes have to deal with aggressive or unhelpful people.

You
- O Good administrative and IT skills.
- O Attention to detail and methodical.
- O Polite and helpful.
- O Good general communication skills.

Entry/learning
- O Some regions have no formal entry requirements, but a good general standard of education or work experience is helpful.
- O You might be asked for at least five GCSEs/S grades (A*–C), A levels or equivalent, or you might need to pass an aptitude test.
- O You can learn on the job, and gain a Level 2 NVQ/SVQ in Administration.

Money
Starting salaries are around £12,000 per year.

Career progress
With experience and qualifications, assistants can become court administrative officers, with salaries from £14,000 to £17,000 per year.

Her Majesty's Courts Service www.hmcourts-service.gov.uk

Trainee legal executive Ⓐ

Working with solicitors and helping them to prepare legal cases

Working for a law firm, usually in a clerical assistant role, while training to become a qualified legal executive. The work involves helping solicitors to prepare court cases, so you could be interviewing people, taking notes, filing, writing letters or researching information.

Pros and cons
- O It can take a long time to go from being a trainee to a qualified person.
- O There are mostly regular working hours.
- O You might need to travel to different courts or police stations.

You
- O Good communication skills.
- O Attention to detail, methodical and organised.

o   Analytical mind and good problem-solver.
o   Discreet and tactful.

Entry/learning

1. There are no minimum academic entry requirements, but at least four GCSEs (A*–C), including English, are recommended. Many entrants have higher qualifications.
2. To become a trainee legal executive, you can apply for clerical work in a law firm and start studying for the first set of City & Guilds/ Ilex Paralegal exams. You can also begin via an apprenticeship.
3. To become a qualified legal executive you must have passed all the ILEX exams, which includes five years' legal employment.

Money
Trainee salaries start at around £12,000 per year.

Career progress
With experience you could end up running your own department or becoming a partner in a law firm. Many people decide to specialise in one subject. You can earn £21,000–£60,000+ per year.

Institute of Legal Executives www.ilex.org.uk

Other jobs to consider

o   Court usher 🚫

o   Legal secretary Ⓐ

o   Politician/Member of Parliament 🚫.

Family 12
Leisure, sport and tourism

Over 600,000 people work in leisure, sport and tourism in the UK. Most of these jobs are about helping people enjoy their leisure time, whether that's getting fit, going on holiday, or visiting a casino or cinema. There are many different employers, from large fitness and travel agent chains, to amusement parks and small independent betting shops and gyms.

Quite a few jobs in this family have no formal entry requirements, but excellent communication skills and customer service skills are usually important. Team work, observation skills, and the ability to follow health and safety rules are important too.

It is common to learn on the job in these different types of work, and there are also apprenticeships where you can gain practical work experience and vocational qualifications at the same time. With experience, many workers progress into supervisory jobs, and some decide to set up their own leisure-related businesses.

Jobs and contacts

Betting shop cashier

Taking bets from customers and paying out winnings

Cashiers in betting shops greet the customers, take bets from them, put up information and displays, oversee the shop and terminals, and pay out winnings. Part of the job involves being alert for criminal activities. You might work for small independent bookmakers or large betting shop chains.

Pros and cons
- It usually involves about 40 working hours per week, but you might have to work until after 10 p.m. on some evenings, or work at weekends.
- You might be responsible for sorting out and safely storing daily cash takings.
- Some customers might be aggressive, threatening, or try to cheat.

You

- Calm, level headed, responsible and trustworthy.
- Good customer service and IT skills.
- Interested in sports.
- Good understanding of shop procedures and safety.

Entry/learning

- You must be aged 18 or over.
- Some jobs have no formal entry requirements but you must have maths skills to handle money and winnings, and good communication skills.
- Most training is on the job.
- Staff can work towards NVQs to gain extra qualifications.

Money

Starting salaries are from £10,500 to £14,000 per year.

Career progress

You can become a shop manager or area manager earning from £15,000 to £45,000+ per year. Some people become self-employed bookmakers, setting up their own independent shops.

Association of British Bookmakers Ltd www.abb.uk.com
Gambling Commission www.gamblingcommission.gov.uk

Fitness instructor/personal trainer

Creating and delivering exercise programmes for classes or individuals

Instructors and trainers help people to reach their fitness goals by leading them through different physical exercises. This training is done in a safe and effective way, and can be given to groups or on a one-to-one basis. Employers can be gyms, leisure centres and health clubs, or trainers can be self-employed.

Pros and cons

- It can be rewarding helping people to reach their fitness goals.
- Working hours can be irregular, with early mornings, late evenings and weekends common times for work.
- If you're self-employed, you need to handle all your finances and promotion.

You

- Fit and well groomed.
- Interest in healthy lifestyles.
- Outgoing, friendly and motivating.
- Understand health and safety issues.

Entry/learning
- There are no formal entry requirements for this job, but you do need good knowledge of fitness training.
- To be placed onto the Register of Exercise Professionals you need to gain a suitable NVQ Level 2 or higher.
- Apprenticeships are available for 16–24 year olds.

Money
Starting salaries are around £12,000 per year.

Career progress
You can become a fitness manager or sports centre manager, or specialise in a certain type of fitness. Wages can be from £14,000 to £30,000+ per year.

Register of Exercise Professionals www.exerciseregister.org
Fitpro www.fitpro.com

Holiday representative

Working in holiday destinations to make sure a travel company's customers have enjoyable and safe trips

Representatives meet holidaymakers at airports and provide information and onward transport to the accommodation. They also hold welcome meetings at resorts and might be responsible for selling tickets for excursions and providing entertainment.

Pros and cons
- You will need to work very long hours, and it can be sometimes physically demanding.
- Work opportunities might be seasonal, with more chances of work in summer.
- You get to work with people of all ages and backgrounds.
- You'll get a chance to travel the world.

You
- Organised with a responsible, mature attitude.
- Great communication skills.
- Friendly, outgoing and able to remain calm under pressure.
- Probably speak another language.

Entry/learning
- There are no specific requirements for some jobs, but a few employers might want certain qualifications or have age restrictions.

o Work experience in customer service can be a great advantage, and so can language skills.
o You can gain qualifications in resort operations at Level 2 or higher, or study for travel and tourism BTECs or AS/A levels.

Money
Starting salaries are around £6,000 per year. Free accommodation and transport are provided.

Career progress
More experienced reps can earn £10,000–£14,000 per year. You can progress into management and earn up to £18,000, or move into sales or customer service roles in the travel industry.

Career in Travel www.careerintravel.co.uk

Leisure centre assistant

Welcoming, helping and supervising customers using leisure centre facilities

Work can vary, but assistants often work on the reception desk selling tickets, making bookings and giving out information. They might also set up, demonstrate and put away equipment for classes, keep the venue clean and tidy, and supervise the use of facilities. Many are qualified first-aiders.

Pros and cons
o The hours might be long, or you might work a rota system that includes weekends.
o The work can involve lifting and carrying and might be tiring sometimes.
o There is usually a friendly atmosphere in the workplace.

You
o Good customer service skills.
o Enjoy working in a team.
o Common sense, responsible attitude to safety.
o Interest in healthy lifestyles.

Entry/learning
o There are no formal entry requirements for many jobs, but some employers might ask for certain GCSEs or other qualifications.
o Most training is on the job, but you can also study NVQs/SVQs or ISRM courses.
o You can also take Royal Life Saving Society qualifications to become a lifeguard.

Money

Starting salaries are around £10,000–£14,000 per year.

Career progress

You can become a team leader, centre manager or area manager, earning £15,500–£35,000+ per year.

Institute of Sport and Recreation Management (ISRM) www.isrm.co.uk
Royal Life Saving Society UK www.lifesavers.org.uk

Interview

Holly, Leisure Centre Assistant,
age 21

'I've been working in an outdoor ski and snowboard centre for three years, since I saw the ad in our local paper and applied. I've been skiing since I was three years old. After working here for five months I got a promotion and now I have extra responsibilities. I oversee health and safety, open up the centre in the morning, lock up at night, handle school bookings and run activity camps. The managers make sure we are trained and up to date, so they arrange regular one to two day courses. This year we have done first aid, child protection and fire safety training.

'Our regular customers are like our friends, they're really into snowsports and we have common interests. There's lots of variety at work. It isn't always perfect, for example it's never nice when you have to clean up sick, and our shifts mean that we work two weekends out of four. But we do have some perks. We get to do free skiing and snowboarding, and we have a generous equipment and clothing allowance where we're allowed to pick our own ski clothes.'

Professional sportsperson

Making a living from competing in team or individual sports

Sports professionals compete at the national and international level in a variety of sports. Very few sportspeople are able to earn a living from sport, even if they compete to a very high standard. Work involves specialised training, keeping fit, playing in competitions, giving interviews and helping to promote your sponsors.

Pros and cons

- The work is highly competitive with few opportunities for sponsorship or employment.
- It is very rewarding, with a chance to excel in your sport.
- An injury can mean the end of a career.
- Most careers are short – you need to have plans for what you will do afterwards.

You

- Outstanding natural ability in your chosen sport.
- Competitive, highly driven and committed.
- Able to stick to training regimes and special diets.
- Pleasant personality and able to work within a team or with the media.

Entry/learning

- No academic qualifications are needed for most sports.
- Apprenticeships and scholarship schemes are available, but only for the most talented or those likely to succeed.

Money

Apprentices earn at least £95 per week, sometimes more.

Career progress

Successful established people working at national and international levels, and winning competitions regularly can earn £20,000 and upwards per year. A few top people earn £100,000+ per year, especially in tennis and football.

Skills Active www.skillsactive.com
Sport England www.sportengland.org

Projectionist

Screening films and operating projectors, mainly working in cinemas

Projectionists operate film screening equipment and make sure that everything runs smoothly during the showing, including the picture and the sound. Some projectionists are also asked to monitor other technical equipment in the cinema, such as lighting. Employers can be multiplexes, small cinema chains, independent or art-house cinemas.

Pros and cons

- The working hours might involve lots of late evenings and weekends.
- It can be very rewarding for film lovers.
- You might be working alone for most of the time and that can get lonely.

You

- Interest in films and cinema.
- Able to operate machinery and keep to timings.
- Good understanding of IT and digital technology.
- Alert to problems if they arise.

Entry/learning

- No specific qualifications are needed for most jobs, but you do need to be aged 18 or over.
- Initial training is on the job.
- You can improve your career prospects by studying part time or taking short courses. This includes the projectionist certificate from BKSTS, or courses run by the National Film and Television School.

Money

Starting salaries are £12,000–£16,000 per year.

Career progress

With experience and qualifications, you can become a senior projectionist earning up to £28,000 per year. Some projectionists move into management.

The Moving Image Society (BKSTS) www.bksts.com
The British Film Institute www.bfi.org.uk

Travel agency salesperson/consultant

Selling travel, accommodation, entertainment and related services to the public

Work mainly involves listening to customers and advising them on their holiday needs. As well as making sales and bookings, the consultant also keeps records and does administrative work. Jobs can be with large or small travel agency chains on the high street, or in call centres.

Pros and cons

- You usually have a standard working week, but you might need to work on Saturdays or work longer days at peak times.
- There are many opportunities for travel and leisure.
- Being kept 'on hold' for long periods during bookings or waiting for internet confirmations can be boring.

You

- Good at selling, outgoing and friendly.
- Excellent organisational and research skills.

- Confident with geography, maths and IT.
- An interest in travel.

Entry/learning

- No formal qualifications are usually required, but good English and maths skills are helpful.
- Most people start work in this area on apprenticeships.
- Training is mostly on the job, and you might be asked to attend short courses.
- You can also gain extra qualifications in travel, tourism and travel agency work, including A levels, diplomas and SQAs, and ABTA certificates.

Money

Starting salaries are around £11,000 per year. You might also get discounts on travel or holidays.

Career progress

You might become an assistant manager or branch manager, earning £15,000–£40,000+ per year. Experienced staff might also move into sales jobs in other areas.

Association of British Travel Agents Limited www.abta.com
Institute of Travel and Tourism www.itt.co.uk

Other jobs to consider

- Croupier/casino worker
- Event/exhibition organiser's assistant Ⓐ
- Lifeguard (see p. 129)
- Nightclub worker
- Theme park assistant
- Tour guide
- Tourist information centre assistant.

Family 13

Marketing, advertising, media, print and publishing

··

About one and a half million people work in these types of jobs, including some who are self-employed. Jobs in this family are broadly about keeping people informed and entertained, sometimes with the aim of selling different products. It can be a very competitive field, so motivation, enthusiasm, networking and work experience are needed if you want to break into these industries.

Some of the jobs are creative, which often involves producing words or images for papers, magazines, books, television programmes and advertisements, and films. Other jobs are about quality control, the production process, communications, management and the business side of these industries. There are also many general and support roles that can suit school leavers, and might lead on to greater responsibilities and more diverse or creative work.

Working hours might sometimes be long and irregular, especially when deadlines and publication or release dates need to be met. Lots of these jobs include opportunities to travel or work on unusual and interesting projects, and many experienced workers set up their own businesses.

Jobs and contacts

Model

Showing off new clothing, accessories, make-up or other products to their best advantage, by wearing them or being near to them

All models are self-employed, and sign up with modelling agencies that find them work. Most agencies have set physical requirements that must be met before a model can be accepted. Work can be indoors in a studio, outdoors on location, at catwalk shows, at conventions, or at sales events.

Pros and cons
- The working hours are irregular and can involve standing for long periods.
- There is intense competition within the industry, and careers are usually over by the age of 30.
- There is a chance to earn well and travel the world.
- Some non-official modelling 'agencies' exploit their clients.

You
- Well groomed and attractive with a good posture.
- Usually expected to be tall and thin to model clothes.
- Professional attitude with good social skills.
- Able to cope with repeated rejections.

Entry/learning
- No specific entry requirements are needed.
- Most training is on the job, although there are some private courses.
- Once working, you should collect a portfolio of flattering pictures to help market yourself for new work.
- If you are aged under 16, you must be licensed to work by your local education and welfare authority.

Money
Starting rates are around £100–£200 per day, but expect the modelling agency to take 20% commission. If you get regular work, your income will be around £10,000–£17,000 per year.

Career progress
A few models with the 'right' looks and skills can earn £40,000–£60,000+ per year. Careers are relatively short, so many models move into model agency booking, management and training, and a few use their knowledge of fashion to design and sell clothes, underwear, and accessories.

Alba Model Information www.albamodel.info
Association of Model Agents www.associationofmodelagents.org

Interview

Jag, Male Model,
aged 20

'I've been modelling for just over a year. I never thought about being a model when I was younger, even though I got approached a few times in the street and talent scouts gave me their cards, I was concentrating on getting my GCSEs and A levels instead and it didn't cross my mind. I have friends at fashion college and last year they had an emergency and asked me to help model at an event in Croydon so I just helped them out. There was a casting with a big agency from London, they said yes and then I had some quick catwalk training and did the show. More work came after that which has really helped with making my portfolio and getting a good range of diverse pictures. I would say *never* pay to get a portfolio done, you don't need to spend money on it, and it won't look that good because you need to be wearing lots of different clothes and be working in a range of locations.

'Casting calls are very specific in their requirements, and you must fit the requirements of the type of modelling you want to go in for – I'm 6 foot 4 and slim, so I do catwalk mainly and some fashion shoots but I'm too tall for many jobs. The money is around £60 to £200 for most jobs but I know people who are more experienced who get paid £7,000 for a weekend's work. I did some work for free when I started out, to make contacts and get some exposure – you never know who's out there watching. I also use model networking sites like Model Mayhem. You have to be really motivated and committed, and you do meet some characters.'

Trainee/assistant photographer

Helping photographers to set up, create and modify photographic images

Assistant photographers help with the whole process of creating photographic pictures. It includes setting up technical lighting, preparing and posing models or objects, using different cameras, and using photo editing and digital enhancing techniques. Work can be in a studio, at an event, or out on location.

Pros and cons
- Working hours tend to be irregular.
- The creative process can be very enjoyable.

o Working to deadlines can be stressful.
o There is strong competition within the industry.

You
o Creative, strong eye for what makes a good picture.
o Self-motivated.
o Good at promoting your work.
o Excellent sales and communication skills.

Entry/learning
o There is no set route for becoming a photographer.
o Many photographers gain qualifications before they start working.
o A portfolio of good quality shots can be very important in finding work.
o Apprenticeships might be available for school leavers.

Money
Trainees can earn around £12,000 per year, with less for apprentices.

Career progress
Experienced photographers tend to specialise in one area, such as fashion, news reporting, weddings or food photography. Wages can be £16,000 to £60,000+ per year. Most photographers are self-employed so their income varies each month.

Association of Photographers www.the-aop.org
Skillset www.skillset.org

Machine printer ⒜

Setting up, checking and running printing machines to make cards, posters, books, brochures, newspapers, etc.

Machine printers oversee the process for manufacturing printed items. This includes setting up and testing machinery such as printing presses, running test batches, troubleshooting and producing final products. A mixture of design skills, computer skills and practical skills are needed.

Pros and cons
o You might have a standard working week but overtime or shift work is common.
o The work involves standing for long periods with some heavy lifting.
o You might need to wear protective equipment such as overalls and ear protectors.
o There might be opportunities to specialise or get promoted.

You
○ Technically minded with an eye for design.
○ Strong attention to detail.
○ Physically fit, good manual skills and normal colour vision.
○ Awareness of health and safety issues.

Entry/learning
○ There are no specific entry requirements, but GCSEs in Maths, a science, Design and Technology and IT are all relevant.
○ Apprenticeships are available.
○ Most training is on the job.
○ Once you are in employment it is possible to study part time for print management qualifications such as HNDs, NVQs or British Printing Industries Federation qualifications.

Money
Starting salaries are around £15,000 per year, with less for apprentices.

Career progress
With experience and qualifications it is possible to specialise in specific types of printing, or become a print production planner or manager, with earnings of £16,000–£60,000 per year. Pay often includes shift allowances or bonuses.

Proskills www.proskills.co.uk/Careers
British Printing Industries Federation www.britishprint.com

Television/film/radio production runner

Providing practical support to other staff during the production of films, television or radio programmes

Television, radio or film runners help out production staff during setting up and filming by carrying out a variety of tasks. These often involve fetching and carrying scripts or other items, running errands, making teas and coffees, bringing food orders to people, taking staff and visitors to different locations, research and administration duties, and cleaning and tidying.

Pros and cons
○ Irregular working hours are common.
○ The job is commonly seen as a stepping stone to other work within film, radio or television.
○ The work is often competitive, yet very tiring and unglamorous.
○ You might need to work to strict deadlines.

You

- Enthusiastic and willing to help.
- Physically fit and work well under pressure.
- Quick thinker and learner.
- Passionate about film, radio or television.

Entry/learning

- There are no set entry requirements, but many entrants do have related degrees.
- Previous work experience can be extremely helpful.
- Enthusiasm and the right attitude are essential.

Money

Work is usually on a freelance basis, with quiet and busy periods. Runners who are in regular work can earn £10,000–£15,000 per year.

Career progress

Runners can become television researchers, production assistants or entry-level assistant film directors. Earnings are variable, but can be around £16,000–£30,000+ per year.

Skillset www.skillset.org

Other jobs to consider

- Advertising installer/bill poster ⊗ Ⓐ
- Camera operator's assistant
- Bookbinder
- Reprographics assistant Ⓐ
- Screen printer.

Family 14

Performing arts

If you work in the performing arts you can be on the stage or the screen, or you can be working behind the scenes. It might seem very glamorous to outsiders, but most of the work involves technical or practical activities, or long rehearsal times, and there is a lot of competition for jobs.

Work in this field can be hard to come by or have irregular hours, but being part of a successful production can be extremely rewarding. Many people in the performing arts are employed on a part-time or project basis, and some successful performers often need to take on more than one job to get by.

There are many opportunities for technical, support, and backstage staff to get promoted, especially with experience and extra study. Performers need to be talented, but must also be highly motivated and able to cope with rejection if they want to succeed.

Jobs and contacts

Actor **A**

Bringing scripts to life by performing on the stage, on film, on radio or television

Acting usually involves bringing fictional characters to life during a performance. Singing and dancing skills might also be needed. Work also includes going to auditions, meeting with agents, learning lines, having costume fittings, and spending time having hair and make-up done.

Pros and cons
- The hours are long and non-standard, often including evenings and weekends.
- People need to get used to being regularly rejected at auditions.
- It can be hard to make a living as a actor as the field is very competitive.
- There is a chance for creative fulfilment, fame and fortune.

You

- o Dedicated with lots of self-discipline.
- o Natural talent plus willingness to learn and train.
- o Good memory (for learning lines).
- o Lots of physical and mental stamina.

Entry/learning

- o There are no set entry requirements, but many entrants have been to drama school or taken drama courses.
- o Experience of working on different productions can be helpful.
- o Some creative apprenticeships are available for performers.
- o Once working, actors must continue to learn and develop new skills as the industry keeps changing.

Money

It is rare for actors to be continuously in work, but it is possible for some to earn around £12,000 per year when starting out.

Career progress

Some actors move into higher profile or long-running roles, earning £14,000–£26,000+ per year. Others might turn to writing, directing or teaching.

Creative & Cultural Skills www.ccskills.org.uk
National Council for Drama Training www.ncdt.co.uk

Lighting technician

Creating a range of lighting effects for performance spaces such as theatre, concerts, advertisements, music videos, film and television

Lighting technicians visit venues before performances, design and set up the lighting effects, fine tune the lighting after watching rehearsals, and operate, maintain and replace equipment. They work closely with set designers and producers to create the right look for the performance, and work alongside sound engineers and technicians.

Pros and cons

- o The hours are irregular, and you will often need to work on evenings and weekends.
- o The results of your work can make you feel proud.
- o You can get to travel and work with interesting people.

You

- o Strong interest in electrical work.
- o Keen interest in drama or music, and visual flair.

- Physically fit, aware of health and safety rules and a head for heights.
- Work well in a team.

Entry/learning

- Lighting technicians must be qualified electricians.
- To start working without already being a qualified electrician, your options are limited to traineeships with specialist companies, or apprenticeships.
- Work experience is very helpful.
- Most training takes place on the job, and it is essential to continue training and gaining new skills throughout your career.

Money

Starting salaries are around £9,500–£10,000 per year.

Career progress

It is possible to become a senior or chief lighting technician, or a technical manager, earning £16,000–£30,000+ per year. Some people move into lighting design, eventually becoming lighting directors.

The Association of British Theatre Technicians www.abtt.org.uk
Creative & Cultural Skills www.ccskills.org.uk

Make-up artist Ⓐ

Applying different types of make-up and styling hair to create specific looks for performers, models and presenters

Make-up artists work in the theatre and at concerts, on film, television, commercial, photographic and video shoots, and at fashion shows. There will be discussions with directors, clients and performers about the desired looks that need to be created, which can include fashion/glamour, ageing, 'natural', injured or fantasy appearances.

Pros and cons

- The working hours can be irregular, often with very early starts or late evenings.
- Seeing your creative vision brought to life can be very satisfying.
- Some cosmetic preparations can cause skin irritations.
- You often need to work under pressure, with tight deadlines.

You

- Creative, with lots of imagination and like creating characters.
- Excellent attention to detail and good technical skills.
- Tactful, friendly and confident.
- Up to date with new developments in hair, make-up and prosthetics.

Entry/learning

o Most make-up artists are trained beauty therapists, with relevant NVQs, VTCT diplomas or other qualifications.
o It is possible to gain entry to this career via an apprenticeship.
o Training is on the job and on short courses.
o Once employed, make-up artists might also undertake specialist make-up design training.

Money

Full-time employees often start on around £15,000 per year, with less for apprentices

Career progress

You can become a senior make-up artist or specialise in particular work such as wigs or prosthetics, earning over £28,000 per year if you are employed full time. Some self-employed make-up artists set up their own backstage team or salon, earning £25,000–£45,000+ if successful.

British Association of Beauty Therapy and Cosmetology Ltd
www.babtac.com
National Association of Screen Make-Up Artists and Hairdressers www. nasmah.co.uk

---

Musician

Performing music for a recording or for the entertainment of a live audience

Musicians can be solo artists, or perform as part of a band, group or orchestra. There are many options, including classical music, popular music, working as a session musician and playing in an armed forces band. Some musicians compose their own material.

Pros and cons

o The hours can be irregular, often with evening and weekend work.
o Performing can be exciting and interesting.
o There are opportunities to travel.
o The work can be hard to come by.

You

o Natural musical talent and a love of music.
o Stamina and determination as the job will require long hours practising.
o Able to cope with criticism and rejection.

Entry/learning

o There are no formal academic requirements for popular music or playing in the armed forces.
o Classical musicians are usually expected to have academic qualifications before

they start work.

o   Most skills are gained on the job and through practice, but some apprenticeships are available.

o   Some musicians have tuition from private tutors, especially vocal training.

Money

There are no average earnings for musicians. Most live gigs pay £50 or more, and session musician rates start at roughly £120 for a job.

Career progress

Very successful and regularly touring, popular artists can earn £500–£2,000+ per week. Some musicians move into teaching, producing or the business side of the music industry.

Creative and Cultural Skills www.ccskills.org.uk
Access to Music www.accesstomusic.co.uk

Sound technician

Creating, transmitting and recording the best quality sound for different types of performances and media

Sound technicians set up and operate a range of technical equipment designed to record or amplify voices, music and other sounds. They might also modify and manipulate these sounds to create the effects that they want. Technicians also test, service, maintain and repair equipment.

Pros and cons

o   There might be standard working hours, or irregular hours with late nights and weekends.

o   The work can be diverse, exciting and interesting.

o   You might be constantly learning new things.

o   You might need to do lots of travel, and working conditions are not always comfortable.

You

o   A love of music and other sound effects.

o   A good ear for pitch and a sense of timing.

o   Understanding of electronics and ICT.

o   Able to concentrate for long periods of time.

Entry/learning

o   No formal qualifications are necessary, although many workers have completed foundation courses or degrees.

o   It is possible to find trainee and assistant posts, and apprenticeships might be available.

o   Work experience is extremely useful.

o Most training is on the job, and continuing professional development is essential to keep up with new technology.

Money
Starting salaries are around £13,000–£18,000 per year, with less for apprentices.

Career progress
You can progress to sound mixer, sound engineer, sound designer or music producer, with top level earnings from £30,000 to £40,000+ per year.

Skillset www.skillset.org
Creative and Cultural Skills www.ccskills.org.uk

Wardrobe assistant Ⓐ

Helping actors and other artists to dress correctly for their performances

Wardrobe assistants mainly work in the theatre, or in film or television, although some work on commercials and music videos. They help to make or buy costumes, and alter, mend and clean them. Assistants also help performers with costume changes during shows, and catalogue and store items afterwards.

Pros and cons
o The hours are irregular and often unsociable.
o There is a chance to be creative and work with clothes.
o You work in an exciting environment.
o There is a lot of competition for jobs.

You
o Good sewing skills, with an eye for detail.
o A love of the performing arts.
o Creative and practical.
o Tactful and calm under pressure.

Entry/learning
o There are no specific entry requirements, but good sewing skills are essential.
o Work experience is very important.
o Once working it is possible to study part time for City & Guilds certificates, BTEC certificates/diplomas and other qualifications.

Money
Starting salaries are around £10,000 per year.

Career progress

More experienced wardrobe assistants can earn £15,000–£20,000+ per year. You can be promoted to wardrobe supervisor or wardrobe master/mistress in a large theatre, earning up to £28,000 per year, or move into costume design or consultancy.

Get Into Theatre www.getintotheatre.org
Creative and Cultural Skills www.ccskills.org.uk

Interview

Suzanna, Theatre Worker,
aged 18

'I do three jobs at my local theatre: front of house assistant, wardrobe assistant and deputy stage manager, and which job depends on the production that we have on. I got into stage management by working as a volunteer assistant stage manager and I love it because everything's fast-paced and fun. During rehearsals it all looks like everything's falling apart but on the first night when it all comes together it's amazing, that's the best bit. You just have to keep going and try to enjoy even the stressful parts, like when nobody can find the props or when organising people seems impossible. The chance to have all this work experience is amazing, and my next step is going to be applying to Rose Bruford College, the specialist performing arts college, where I want to study for their Stage Management MA.'

Other jobs to consider

- DJ
- Entertainer ⊗ Ⓐ
- Props maker's assistant Ⓐ
- Roadie
- Set carpenter/painter/plasterer Ⓐ
- Singer
- Stagehand Ⓐ
- Theatre production assistant Ⓐ.

Family 15

Personal and cleaning services, including hair and beauty

Most of these jobs are about helping people to look their best, or making working and living environments safe and hygienic. All of them need a level of customer service, and many jobs are open to school leavers.

UK employment statistics

Hair and beauty: 240,000+ people

Funeral industry: 16,000 people

Cleaning sector: 700,000 people

Many workers in these industries start out as trainees or apprentices, and fit studying for vocational qualifications around their paid work. With experience, it is possible to progress into management or senior technician positions, and many workers also set up their own businesses such as cleaning firms or beauty salons.

Jobs and contacts

Beauty consultant

Promoting and selling beauty products to customers, and giving advice

Includes recommending products to customers, giving makeovers and demonstrations, managing stock levels and handling payments. Work is mainly in shops, department stores, airports, spas and hotels. Most consultants are employees, but some are self-employed and work from home.

Pros and cons
- There is a possibility of flexible working hours.
- You can get free/discounted products.
- You might be on your feet all day.
- Self-employed people need to control their finances and marketing, and tend to need a car and driving licence.

You
- Good communication, sales and social skills.
- Well groomed and smart.
- Up to date with beauty products and fashions.
- An eye for design and what suits people.

Entry/learning
- There are no specific requirements. Entry might be via apprenticeships in Retail, or Diploma in Hair & Beauty Studies.
- Learning is mostly in the workplace or on company training courses.
- You can work towards a Level 2 BTEC Award, Certificate or Diploma in Retail Skills, or other qualifications.

Money
Salaries start at £11,000–£13,000 per year. You might earn extra commission on sales.

Career progress
You could become a team manager, account manager or area manager, earning £20,000–£30,000+ per year.

Skillsmart Retail Ltd www.skillsmartretail.com

Beauty therapist

Carrying out a range of face and body treatments to improve the appearance or well-being of clients

Work might include giving facials, massages, fake tans, electrolysis, waxing and other treatments. Sites include beauty salons and clinics, hotels, health clubs and health farms. Beauty therapists need to clean up after their clients, handle products safely, and keep client records. A few visit clients in their homes or workplaces.

Pros and cons
- You could have flexible working hours.
- The perks can include free/cheaper beauty products, gym membership or accommodation.

- The work is physically demanding, with much standing and bending.
- Self-employed people need to control their finances and marketing, and might need a car and driving licence.

You

- Calm, friendly and a good listener.
- Enjoy helping people.
- Well groomed with good personal hygiene.
- Physically fit.
- Understand the importance of safety and cleanliness.

Entry/learning

- There are no set entry requirements, but you are often expected to have a Level 3 qualification, or be doing Skillseekers training or an apprenticeship.
- The Diploma in Hair and Beauty Studies might be useful.
- Trainees often work towards Level 2/3 NVQs/SVQs in Beauty Therapy at colleges or a private beauty school.
- Advanced learning is available as HNC/HND/foundation degree/degree in Beauty Therapy.

Money

Salaries start at £10,000–£11,000 per year.

Career progress

You could move into management, or set up your own salon. Some people expand into holistic and alternative therapies. You can also become a trainer, lecturer or health/beauty sales representative. You could earn up to £16,000–£20,000+ per year.

British Association of Beauty Therapy and Cosmetology
www.babtac.com
Hairdressing and Beauty Industry Authority www.habia.org
Guild of Professional Beauty Therapists Ltd (GPBT)
www.beautyguild.com

Hairdresser/barber

Shampooing, cutting, dyeing, and styling clients' hair, and providing other beauty services and advice

Most trainee hairdressers work in salons, either small businesses or branches of larger chains. Hairdressers and barbers discuss appearance and give advice to their clients, and carry out a range of services from cutting and styling to tinting. They sweep and clear up after their clients, and prepare equipment and chemicals.

Pros and cons

- There is a sociable atmosphere, with a chance to be creative.
- You will need to be physically fit, as there is much standing and bending.
- You often need to work long hours, including weekends.
- Hairdressing chemicals can be a problem for people with skin conditions or allergies.

You

- Friendly with good communication skills.
- An eye for fashion, and some creative flair.
- Work well with your hands.
- Able to run a reception desk at busy times.

Entry/learning

- There are no minimum entry requirements for this job, and you can start as a junior assistant.
- You can sign up for apprenticeships and Skillseekers.
- The Diploma in Hair and Beauty Studies might be useful.
- Most hairdressers do extra training, such as NVQs/SVQs at Levels 1–3, and other more specialised courses.

Money

Salaries start at around £8,000–£11,000 per year, and you might get tips from customers. Experienced hairdressers can earn £20,000–£30,000+ per year.

Career progress

You can become a senior stylist, a salon manager or a hairdressing trainer. Some people set up their own salon or mobile service, or specialise in colouring techniques or hair extensions.

Hairdressing And Beauty Industry Authority www.habia.org
The Hairdressing Council www.haircouncil.org.uk

Interview

Emma, Apprentice Hairdresser, age 17

'I was always obsessed with hairstyles and make-up – at school I was always doing my friends' hair and I still do it now because some of them come in on model nights! I decided to start a Level 2 apprenticeship and was lucky to get taken on by a branch of a big hairdressing chain. OK, the pay isn't brilliant and I'm tired after work sometimes, but it's a really friendly team and I'm learning lots. When you start out you spend a lot of time sweeping or washing up mixing bowls, sitting on reception, washing hair, doing laundry, stuff like that, but it gets better. It's a big company so I want to work my way up.'

Image consultant/personal shopper

Advising people on how to make the most of their appearance by selecting clothes, accessories and make-up

Personal shoppers consult with clients to find out what image they want to project, then help them to pick out the right items to suit their lifestyle, body shape, skin tone and budget. Image consultants also help with confidence, body language and communication skills. Most work is done with private clients, although some personal shoppers work for department stores.

Pros and cons
- There might be flexible working hours, or you might have to work evenings or weekends.
- There is a chance to help people, and be creative.
- There's lots of competition for the work, and it's hard to get a promotion.

You
- Well groomed and confident.
- Good communication skills.
- Very tactful, but honest.
- Strong interest in fashion, an eye for design and colour.

Entry/learning
- There are no specific entry requirements, but fashion retail work or hairdressing experience can be an advantage.
- You can also study image consultancy, beauty therapy, marketing or media qualifications to help your career.

Money
New full-time employees can earn £10,000–£15,000 per year, rising to £30,000+ with experience.

Career progress

Self-employed people can grow their businesses over time, or break into the corporate or media markets, which often pay best.

Federation of Image Consultants www.tfic.org.uk

Nail technician

Caring for hands and nails, and sometimes providing nail extensions and nail art

Nail technicians are employed by over 17,000 businesses in the UK, such as nail bars, hair and beauty salons, hotels, spas, airports, shopping centres and hospitals. They might provide a range of treatments to their clients including manicures and pedicures, nail repairs and extensions, nail art and jewellery. They clean and tidy up after each client, and might work with chemicals, stencils and airbrushes.

Pros and cons

- The working hours might be flexible, or there might be some unsocial hours.
- You might get free/reduced beauty treatments.
- The products and chemicals might be unsuitable for people with skin conditions or allergies.

You

- Friendly and well groomed.
- Good understanding of health and hygiene.
- Able to work quickly and accurately with your hands.
- An eye for design and interest in fashion.

Entry/learning

- There are no set entry requirements, *but* some local environmental health departments might insist that nail businesses are licensed – this means you will have to have a recognised qualification such as an NVQ/SVQ.
- Entry can also be via Skillseekers and apprenticeships.
- For keeping workers up to date, product manufacturers regularly run short courses.
- More training includes NVQs/SVQs, or BTEC Diplomas and Certificates in Nail Treatments, Nail Technology or Nail Art.

Money

Entry-level salary is around £10,000–£11,000 per year. Some salons offer bonus schemes and commission.

Career progress

With experience and qualifications you could become a salon manager, earning up to £28,000 a year, or set up your own business.

British Association of Beauty Therapy and Cosmetology www.babtac.com
The Association of Nail Technicians Tel: 020 7812 3724

Other jobs to consider

- Body piercer
- Spa therapist **A**
- Tattoo artist
- Wedding planner
- Wigmaker.

Crematorium technician

Assisting with the running of a crematorium, and escorting mourners in and out of the chapel

Crematorium technicians usually work for local councils, and learn on the job while they are working. The number of cremations each year is increasing. Trainee technicians clean and prepare the chapel and crematorium, and escort the funeral party in and out of the chapel. After the ceremony they assist with operating the cremation equipment, and the correct storage and disposal of human remains.

Pros and cons

- You usually have a standard working week, perhaps with some occasional overtime.
- The work can be physically tiring.
- You might need a strong stomach for some tasks.
- It can be challenging dealing with people who are grieving.

You

- Physically fit with good practical skills.
- Sensitive and tactful when dealing with bereaved people.
- Mature and responsible attitude.
- Able to follow health and safety instructions.

Entry/learning
- There are no formal qualifications needed to start work.
- To work unsupervised you must become qualified.
- To become qualified you must complete the Institute of Cemetery and Crematorium Management's BTEC Accredited Cremator Technicians Training Scheme, or the Federation of Burial and Cremation Authorities' TEST Scheme.

Money
Salaries start at £11,000–£12,000 per year.

Career progress
With qualifications and experience, you can progress to management positions, with wages from £20,000 to £25,000 per year.

Institute of Cemetery and Crematorium Management
www.iccm-uk.com
Federation of Burial and Cremation Authorities www.fbca.org.uk

---

Embalmer

Preparing the bodies of dead people for funerals, and for viewing by their relatives

Most embalmers work in operating rooms at funeral parlours. They work with dead bodies, draining them of blood and gases, and replacing them with disinfecting fluid. They wash and dry the bodies and hair of the deceased, and sometimes restore parts of the body if there have been severe injuries, or add make-up.

Pros and cons
- There is constant demand for embalmers.
- The work is physically hard and there might be irregular work hours.
- The work is carried out in a cold environment with dangerous or irritating chemicals.

You
- Respectful, mature and professional.
- Not squeamish.
- Good at handling tools and medical equipment.
- Able to work to a very high standard of hygiene.

Entry/learning
- There are no formal entry requirements, but an understanding of science might be useful.

o   Most training is on the job.
o   Trainees also tend to have part-time tuition, and study for qualifications from the International Examinations Board of Embalmers.

Money
Starting salaries are from £12,500 per year.

Career progress
Embalmers can gain manager status or become self-employed. With experience and training some earn £20,000–£30,000 per year.

British Institute of Embalmers www.bioe.co.uk

Funeral service operative

Working for a funeral director, making practical arrangements for funerals and cremations, and attending funeral services

Funeral service operatives offer advice to families of the deceased, and take note of the details they want included in the funeral ceremony. They then provide the practical arrangements for the funeral, such as arranging times and dates with churches, crematoriums and cemeteries. They also prepare the body of the dead person for burial, and arrange transport, flowers and catering.

Pros and cons
o   Many operatives like helping people and find this work personally rewarding.
o   The business is permanently on call, so you might have to work a rota or shifts, with some irregular hours.
o   It can be challenging dealing with people who are grieving.

You
o   Smartly dressed, usually in a suit.
o   Tactful, mature and sensitive.
o   Good communication and organisation skills.
o   Careful when completing paperwork.

Entry/learning
o   There are no minimum entry requirements, and most operatives learn from practical experience while they are working.
o   For driving duties, a driving licence is needed.
o   You can gain funeral services qualifications such as NVQs/SVQs at Levels 2–4, the National Association of Funeral Directors' foundation certificate, or BTEC/SQA certificates.

- Advanced qualifications include funeral-related management training, and studies to become a funeral director.

Money
Starting salaries are around £12,500–£14,000 per year.

Career progress
If you work for a larger organisation you might become a branch, area or regional manager. At senior or management level, you could earn £30,000+ per year. Some experienced people set up their own business.

The British Institute of Funeral Directors www.bifd.org.uk
National Association of Funeral Directors www.nafd.org.uk

Other jobs to consider

- Cemetery worker.

Car valet

Cleaning and polishing the inside and outside of cars and other vehicles

The work involves using specialist equipment to wash down the outside of cars, and clean and polish everything from seats to windows to tyres. It also involves cleaning inside cars, and shampooing carpets and upholstery. Car valets work for vehicle service centres, new and used car dealerships, car rental companies, and valeting businesses.

Pros and cons
- You will usually be working outside in all types of weather.
- The work involves lots of standing, bending and reaching, and you will be working in dirty or messy conditions.
- Working hours are often flexible.
- You will come into regular contact with cleaning chemicals, so the work might not be suitable if you have skin conditions or allergies.

You
- Good customer service skills.
- Reliable and work well in a team.
- Fast and thorough, with an eye for detail.

- Physically fit.
- Understand health and safety issues.

Entry/learning
- No qualifications are needed for this work, and you usually learn on the job.
- For most jobs you need to be at least 17 years old and have a driving licence.
- Manufacturers of cleaning products might offer short courses.
- You might wish to complete the Car Valeting Certificate from the British Institute of Cleaning Science, or NVQ/SVQ Level 1 in Vehicle Maintenance.

Money
Starting salaries are £10,500–£12,000 per year.

Career progress
With experience and overtime work you could earn £17,000–£24,000 per year. Some valets set up their own business.

Asset Skills www.assetskills.org
British Institute of Cleaning Science www.bics.org.uk

Caretaker/maintenance person

Maintaining buildings and their grounds, including schools, colleges, factories or office blocks

Caretakers work indoors and outdoors, checking that everything in a building is clean, tidy and working properly. They are usually responsible for unlocking and locking buildings at the start and end of each day, carrying out small maintenance jobs, and reporting large maintenance jobs. The work also often involves gardening and cleaning duties.

Pros and cons
- You might be on call, or have to work early mornings or late evenings.
- The work is physically demanding.
- You must understand how to use ladders and other equipment safely.
- You will need to be working with cleaning chemicals, and might need to wear protective clothing.

You
- Responsible, reliable, honest, practical.
- Good communication skills.
- Able to work without constant supervision.
- Physically fit.

Entry/learning
- No qualifications are needed, but experience in basic DIY can be useful.
- Most training is on the job.
- You might wish to study for an NVQ Level 3 in Property and Caretaking Supervision.

Money
Starting salaries range from £11,000 to £14,500 per year.

Career progress
With experience you could become a team manager or senior caretaker, with wages from £16,000–£25,000+ per year. Some caretakers set up their own mobile businesses.

Asset Skills www.assetskills.org
Chartered Institute of Housing www.cih.org
The Caretakers' Website www.thecaretakers.net

Chimney sweep

Inspecting and cleaning chimneys and flues, and heating appliances and vents

Chimney sweeps inspect, clean and service the flues and chimneys of open fires, and heating and cooking appliances. They also give reports to their customers, including advice about maintenance or urgent work needed, and suggested dates for the next inspection. Most of the work is in people's homes, but there might also be work at factories and other places.

Pros and cons
- Most of the work is done alone.
- It can be full or part time, with extra hours in spring or autumn.
- The work is often dirty and messy.
- Protective clothing is needed, including equipment to protect your lungs.

You
- Good customer service skills and a professional attitude.
- Understanding of health and safety issues.
- Practical and able to use a range of tools.
- Physically fit and enjoy practical work.

Entry/learning
- There are no formal entry requirements, and most people are trained on the job.
- A driving licence is usually needed.

- Trainees can complete a National Association of Chimney Sweeps induction course to gain probationary membership.
- You can also complete a City & Guilds qualification in Chimney Cleaning and an entrance exam to join the Guild of Master Sweeps.

Money
There are no set rates of pay, but full-time workers can earn around £16,000 per year.

Career progress
Most chimney sweeps become self-employed, working alone or in pairs, charging £30 to £55 per hour.

National Association of Chimney Sweeps www.chimneyworks.com
Guild of Master Sweeps www.guildofmasterchimneysweeps.co.uk

Cleaner (domestic/office)

Tidying and cleaning buildings and other places where people live, work or visit

Cleaners use cleaning products and equipment to keep buildings, trains or planes tidy and hygienic for the people who use them. Duties usually include removing rubbish, dusting, mopping floors, vacuuming, polishing, disinfecting kitchens and bathrooms, and cleaning windows. There is a shortage of skilled cleaners in some areas.

Pros and cons
- The hours can vary, but might involve early mornings or late nights.
- You will be dealing with dirty and messy conditions daily.
- You often work in a team, which can be sociable and enjoyable.
- Cleaning chemicals can be unsuitable for people with some skin conditions or allergies.

You
- Motivated, practical and trustworthy.
- Physically fit.
- Able to operate cleaning appliances and other equipment.
- Good understanding of health and safety issues.

Entry/learning
- There are no formal entry requirements, most training is carried out while working.
- Relevant qualifications include NVQs/SVQs at Levels 1 and 2, British Institute of Cleaning Science qualifications, or apprenticeships in Cleaning and Support Services.

Money
Starting salaries can be from £10,000 to £11,000 per year.

Career progress
Many cleaners become specialist cleaners or managers earning £20,000+ per year, or set up their own business.

Asset Skills www.assetskills.org
British Institute of Cleaning Science www.bics.org.uk

Dry cleaning/laundry operative

Serving customers, and putting clothes and other items through laundry or dry-cleaning processes

Operatives launder or dry clean clothes or items such as bed linen, hospital linen, towels and restaurant table linen. Work includes sorting, cleaning, drying, ironing and packing different items. Operatives might also serve customers and process payments. Most laundries and dry cleaning businesses are found in urban areas, and might sometimes be attached to hotels, hospitals or prisons.

Pros and cons
- The work might include late hours, or weekends.
- Conditions are often hot, humid and noisy.
- The work can be physically tiring.
- Exposure to detergents or other chemicals might be unsuitable for people with skin conditions or allergies.

You
- Work well in a team.
- Understand health and safety issues.
- Good customer care skills.
- Motivated and reliable.
- Good eye for detail.

Entry/learning
- No qualifications are needed, and training usually takes place on the job.
- You can study for NVQs/SVQs or practical laundry certificates from the Guild of Cleaners and Launderers, or do an apprenticeship.

Money
Starting salaries are from £11,500 to £12,500 per year.

Career progress

With experience you could become a supervisor or manager, earning from £16,500 to £30,000 per year. Some people specialise in cleaning or mending delicate fabrics.

Guild of Cleaners and Launderers www.gcl.org.uk
Textile Services Association www.tsa-uk.org

Pest control technician

Assessing and removing infestations of unwanted insects and other animals (vermin)

Pest control technicians find and remove a variety of creatures including rats, mice, rabbits, birds, fleas, cockroaches, wasps and other insects. They often use specialist equipment and toxic chemicals. They give advice to their clients about the problem. Employers can be councils, small businesses or national organisations.

Pros and cons
- You might need to work overtime or be able to work flexible hours.
- The work involves lots of travelling.
- You need to wear protective clothing.
- Gases and other toxic chemicals can be a problem if you have asthma or allergies.

You
- Follow health and safety instructions carefully.
- Good customer service skills.
- Stay calm in dirty and unpleasant situations.
- Humane approach to destruction of animals.

Entry/learning
- No specific qualifications are needed to start, and training takes place on the job.
- You can study pest control at various levels, starting with the British Pest Control Promotion of Health Certificate, a Level 2 qualification.

Money

Starting salaries are from £12,000 to £14,500 per year.

Career progress

With experience and qualifications it is possible to become a manager or supervisor, earning £25,000 to £30,000+ per year. Some people set up their own businesses.

British Pest Control Association www.bpca.org.uk

Recycling/refuse/waste management operative ⊘ Ⓐ

Collecting rubbish and unwanted items and taking them to an official tip or recycling depot

Operatives collect waste from homes and workplaces, and deliver it to tips or other official waste management depots. They might also help to sort items for recycling, or drive a lorry or van. Jobs are mainly with local councils, contractors working for local councils or recycling companies.

Pros and cons
- Most work starts early in the morning and finishes mid-afternoon.
- Protective clothing is needed.
- The work can be smelly and dirty.
- You need to be 18 to do most of these jobs.

You
- Work well in a team.
- Physically fit.
- Strong stomach, and don't mind getting your hands dirty.
- Follow health and safety instructions.

Entry/learning
- No qualifications are needed to start, health and safety courses are available and other training is done on the job.
- An HGV licence is needed to drive a refuse lorry.
- Apprenticeships/Skillseekers are available.
- NVQs/SVQs are available at Levels 1–3 in Waste Management or Recycling Operations.

Money
Salaries start at around £11,000 per year for loaders, and drivers can earn £17,000–£20,000.

Career progress
In time you can become a team leader, supervisor or manager. Senior jobs can pay £18,000–£25,000+ per year.

Waste Management Industry Training and Advisory Board
www.wamitab.org.uk

Other jobs to consider

- Carpet/upholstery cleaner
- Hospital cleaner **A**
- Industrial cleaner
- Street cleaner **A**
- Window cleaner **A**.

Family 16

Retail, sales and customer services

....

Over three million people work in the retail industry in the UK, and all the jobs within it need excellent communication skills, because staff need to keep customers happy. A further 800,000 people work in customer services, including contact centres. There are many opportunities for school leavers in this job family, which employs over 12% of the whole UK workforce.

Customers are usually the general public, but there are some more specialised jobs that involve dealing with buyers from a particular trade. Work mainly takes place in shops and other sales environments such as markets, but there are also office-based jobs and telephone-based jobs. Most employees work about 37–40 hours per week, but some types of work involve extra hours in the evenings or at weekends, or doing shifts. It might be possible to earn extra money by working overtime, or earning bonuses or a commission.

If you are a business-minded person, there are many opportunities for promotion. Many staff work their way up to become team leaders, supervisors or managers. In larger organisations, it is also possible to move into different departments, including administration and finance, which often involves extra training and study.

Jobs and contacts

Builders' merchant's assistant

Selling building and DIY materials to the construction trade and/or to the public

Builders' merchant's assistants handle and sell a variety of stock including bricks, timber, bathroom units, tools, cement, and painting and decorating materials. They also deal with customer enquiries, check invoices and arrange deliveries. Employers include independent businesses, specialist and trade suppliers, and large DIY retail chains.

Pros and cons

- You usually have a fairly standard working week, but often you might be working at weekends and starting early in the morning.
- The work can be very physical and involve heavy lifting, ladders and forklift trucks.
- There is lots of paperwork to take care of.
- You often work outside in all weather conditions.

You

- Good customer service and IT skills.
- Physically fit and healthy.
- Good with numbers and paperwork.
- Follow health and safety instructions.

Entry/learning

- There are no set entry requirements, but having GCSE English and Maths can be useful and some of the newer diplomas might be relevant, as is retail experience.
- Different apprenticeships are available.
- Most training is on the job.
- You can study part time for NVQs/SVQs in Distribution and Warehousing, Customer Service, Retail, or Business and Administration.

Money

Starting salaries are around £12,000 per year.

Career progress

You can progress to supervisor or manager, earning £20,000–£50,000+ per year. Some people move into related areas such as administration, warehousing or sales representative work.

Builders Merchants Federation www.bmf.org.uk

Butcher (retail) Ⓐ Ⓐ⁺

Preparing and selling a range of meat and poultry products

Butchers prepare meat and poultry carcasses for sale by cutting, jointing, de-boning, trimming and slicing them. They might also prepare mince, diced meat, and burgers and sausages. Work is mainly in supermarkets, large chains or small butchers' shops, and there are also some employment opportunities in the wholesale trade.

Pros and cons

- Most butchers have regular working hours, including Saturday work and being ready for 7 a.m. deliveries.
- Work is mainly in a butcher's shop or behind a supermarket counter, and in chilled storage areas.
- The work involves a lot of standing, physical work and heavy lifting.
- There is a risk of injury from machinery, knives and tools.

You

- Practical, physically fit, and careful with tools.
- Strong respect for health and safety, and food hygiene.
- Customer service skills.
- Able to handle cash and other payments.

Entry/learning

- No set qualifications are needed, but maths and English skills are important; some employers ask for GCSEs or set aptitude tests.
- Previous work experience in retail or the food and drink industry can be useful.
- Apprenticeships and advanced apprenticeships are available.
- Most employers offer on-the-job training and short courses, and you can study for NVQs in meat and poultry processing or for Meat Training Council certificates.

Money

Most apprentice butchers start out on around £8,000 per year.

Career progress

It is possible to progress into more skilled and senior roles, including supervisor, earning £11,000–£36,000 per year. Some butchers also set up their own shops or specialist businesses, selling to the catering trade or the public.

The Meat Training Council www.meattraining.org.uk

Checkout operator Ⓐ

Operating a till in a shop and taking payments for goods

Checkout operators are employed by supermarkets and other stores and retail outlets. They sit at tills, scanning and weighing goods, or entering prices using a keypad. They remove security tags and might help to pack or bag up the products, then take payments and vouchers, process store cards and give cashback and receipts.

Pros and cons

- There might be flexible working hours, and opportunities for overtime.
- The work involves sitting for long periods, and wearing a uniform.
- The work can often be routine or repetitive.
- There are often staff discounts or other perks.

You

- Quick and accurate when you work.
- Customer service skills.
- Able to handle cash and other payments correctly.
- Calm and efficient under pressure.

Entry/learning

- There are no set entry requirements but employers usually want GCSEs (A–C) or equivalent in English and Maths, and might ask you to take a maths test.
- Apprenticeships are available.
- Most training is done on the job.
- You can study for Levels 1–3 NVQs/SVQs related to retail, or BTEC First and National qualifications.

Money

Starting salaries are around £11,000–£12,000 per year.

Career progress

Pay increases with experience and you can also become a supervisor, earning £14,500–£22,000 per year.

Skillsmart Retail Ltd www.skillsmartretail.com

Interview

Liz, Supermarket Checkout Operator, age 18

'It took ages to find a job, and I struggled to get one because I didn't have a lot of GCSEs. I spent ages looking in the paper and online, then one day I was shopping in this supermarket and I had an idea. I asked if they had any vacancies at the checkout and they said some people were leaving soon. They put my CV on file and called two weeks later. They went on what they saw at the interview and didn't ask me for specific exam results. They're a nice team and I've been here two years now.

'The work takes up a lot of time – it's my first job and took some getting used to. We work shifts but they are flexible with the hours most of the time, so I can go to college part time too. I'm doing AS levels now and one day I would like to do a business degree. We get training as well, like customer service DVDs, meetings, till training, and lots of health and safety. Sometimes we get rude customers but you just have to be polite and deal with it. Thursdays, Fridays and Saturdays are the busiest and I always do some work on the Saturday. Mostly I'm sat working on the till, but if my shift is one after the store has closed to customers then I have to tidy up the store and put stock out on the shelves and in the freezers.'

Contact (call) centre operative

Dealing with customers over the telephone, based in a call centre office

Contact centre operatives do a range of telephone-based work, which can include customer care, handling complaints, carrying out market research, or selling or promoting goods and services. While talking to customers, operatives have to find and input information onto computers.

Pros and cons
- The work is office based and might involve shifts covering nights, evenings or weekends.
- You are usually given work targets to work towards, which can be stressful, but if you meet your targets you can be paid a bonus.
- Some customers might be angry, impatient or insulting.
- Your work might be heavily monitored by supervisors.

You
- Excellent customer service skills.
- Quick and efficient when using IT.
- Work well in a team.
- Calm under pressure.

Entry/learning
- There are no formal qualifications, but many employers will ask for GCSEs in Maths and English, or Level 1 or 2 qualifications.
- Most training takes place on the job and on courses run by employers.
- It is possible to study part time for NVQs/SVQs in Customer Service, Contact Centre Skills and other related subjects.

Money

Starting salaries are around £13,500 per year and you might also be paid performance-related bonuses or commission.

Career progress

It is possible to progress to team leader, supervisor or manager, earning £16,000–£25,000+ per year. Experienced staff might also take on training roles.

Institute of Customer Service www.instituteofcustomerservice.com

Customer service assistant Ⓐ

Selling products or services, or providing help and information to customers

Assistants deal directly with customers, whether face to face, by email or by telephone. The nature of their work varies according to their employer and department, but can include resolving problems, answering questions or giving out information, dealing with complaints, or selling products and services.

Pros and cons

- You usually have a standard working week, but some jobs require shift work, or evenings or weekends.
- You will be sitting at a desk with a headset and computer, or standing behind a store desk for most of the day.
- Helping people can be satisfying.
- Some customers might be angry, frustrated or rude.

You

- Polite, with excellent interpersonal skills.
- Patient and calm under pressure.
- Understand the needs of your customers.

Entry/learning

- No set qualifications needed, but employers often ask for four or more GCSEs (A–C), or other Level 1 or 2 qualifications, or higher, and previous customer service or retail experience is an advantage.
- Apprenticeships are available.
- Training is often done on the job, and some organisations offer management training schemes.
- You can also study part time for Levels 1–4 NVQs/SVQs and awards from the Institute of Customer Service.

Money
Starting salaries are around £10,000–£12,000 per year.

Career progress
You can progress to supervisory or management roles, earning £16,000–£40,000+ per year.

Institute of Customer Service www.instituteofcustomerservice.com

---

Florist

Designing, creating and selling floral gifts and displays

Florists use flowers and other plants and materials to make up bouquets and other floral arrangements and displays. They also advise customers on suitable designs and prices, and take payments. Some florists deliver in person to their customers, or set up displays at events.

Pros and cons
○ You will usually be working in a shop with standard working hours, but you might need to work at weekends or have early starts.
○ The work involves standing for most of the day.
○ There is a chance to be creative on a daily basis.

You
○ Know about plants and flowers, with no allergies to them.
○ Creative, with an eye for shape and design.
○ Practical skills, including delicate manual work.
○ Good customer service skills and an excellent listener.

Entry/learning
○ There are no set entry requirements, but English and money skills are needed, and crafts and retail experience are an advantage.
○ Apprenticeships are available.
○ Most training takes place on the job.
○ You can also study for floristry qualifications such as Levels 2–3 NVQs, and BTEC certificates and diplomas.

Money
Starting salaries are usually the national minimum wage, reaching £18,000 per year with more experience.

Career progress

It is possible to move into management or become self-employed, earning around £25,000 per year. Some businesses specialise in providing flowers for offices and restaurants, or for weddings or funerals.

British Florist Association www.britishfloristassociation.org
Lantra Careers www.afuturein.com

Meat hygiene inspector

Making sure that meat production meets strict legal and hygiene standards

Inspectors visit animal breeders, slaughterhouses, meat stores and processing plants to make sure that meat and poultry are safe to eat. You work in teams and report to an official veterinarian. Work also includes writing up reports, and making sure that unsafe or unwanted meat is destroyed safely.

Pros and cons
- You usually have a standard working week, but there might be some emergency call-outs or weekend work.
- The work involves lots of travelling to slaughterhouses, meat processing plants, poultry and cattle farms.
- Protective clothing is needed, and you will be using sharp tools and equipment.
- The work can be cold, noisy and smelly.

You
- Excellent communication skills.
- Understanding of relevant laws and hygiene regulations.
- Observant and calm.
- Physically fit and healthy.

Entry/learning
- You must have a Royal Society for Public Health Level 3 Certificate in Meat Hygiene and Inspection before you can work.
- School leavers who do not have this certificate can apply for apprenticeships.
- Once trained/qualified, inspectors must take regular courses to refresh their knowledge and learn about new developments.
- It is also possible to take extra qualifications to become a manager or senior inspector.

Money
Trainees earn around £17,000 per year, rising to around £22,000 with experience.

Career progress

It is possible to become a senior meat inspector, earning £24,000–£33,000 per year.

Royal Society for Public Health www.rsph.org.uk
FSA Meat Hygiene Service
www.food.gov.uk/foodindustry/meat/mhservice/

Sales/retail assistant

Helping customers to choose goods or services, and taking their payments

Retail assistants' work can vary according to their employer and department. Most work directly with customers, demonstrating and selling goods, and operating tills to take payments or give refunds. They might also arrange deliveries, deal with complaints, keep sales areas tidy and re-stock shelves.

Pros and cons

- Most assistants have regular working hours, which might include weekends or evenings.
- You meet a variety of people every day.
- The work involves lots of standing and possibly carrying.
- Some customers can be frustrated or angry.

You

- Well groomed, friendly and helpful.
- Calm when under pressure.
- Able to deal politely with difficult people.
- Able to handle cash and other payments.

Entry/learning

- No specific qualifications are needed, but some employers might ask for two to four GCSEs (A–C) or equivalent, or ask you to take tests in basic English or maths.
- Apprenticeships and advanced apprenticeships are available.
- Once you're working there are several NVQs/SVQs you can study for part time.

Money

Starting salaries are around £11,000–£12,000 per year in most jobs.

Career progress

You can progress to working as a supervisor, earning £19,000–£22,000 per year. You might be paid bonuses or commission for sales.

Skillsmart Retail Ltd www.skillsmartretail.com
British Shops and Stores Association www.bssa.co.uk

Stock control assistant

Refilling shelves and displays in a supermarket or other retail environment

Stock control assistants might work while stores are open, or after they're closed for the evening. They help to keep shelves and displays tidy and full of stock, and rotate stock so that the newest items sell last. They might also have to help customers with enquiries about the store's products.

Pros and cons

- There are usually regular working hours, with some evening and weekend work included.
- You can be on your feet all day, and there might be heavy lifting and carrying to do.
- Most workers have to wear a uniform.
- It can be difficult to gain promotion without taking extra qualifications.

You

- Physically fit.
- Able to work unsupervised.
- Approachable and helpful.
- A good team worker.

Entry/learning

- There are no set entry requirements, but some employers will ask for GCSEs (A–E) or equivalent in English and Maths.
- A hard-working attitude and previous customer service experience are both helpful.
- Apprenticeships are available.
- Most training is on the job, and you can also study part time for NVQs and other retail or customer service qualifications.

Money

Starting salaries are around £10,000 per year, up to around £15,000 with more experience.

Career progress

It is possible to become a checkout operator or move into team leader or supervisory roles, earning up to £18,000 per year.

British Shops and Stores Association www.bssa.co.uk
Skillsmart Retail Ltd www.skillsmartretail.com

Other jobs to consider

- Car salesperson **A**
- Filling station sales assistant
- Fishmonger
- Greengrocer
- Jeweller **A**
- Market trader
- Meter reader
- Post office clerk **A**
- Shoe repairer
- Vehicle parts operative **A**
- Wine merchant

Family 17

Science, mathematics and statistics

....

Most jobs in this sector are at the technician and professional levels. There are only a few job opportunities for the youngest school leavers, and your options will be better if you are 18 years old and have A levels or equivalent qualifications. There are some apprenticeships available for those aged 16 and over.

Jobs in this family involve observation, experiments and research to learn new things, improve products, and solve problems. Workers need to be organised, logical, good with numbers, and having an enquiring mind is important. Employers include government departments, academic research centres, health services, charities and commercial companies.

With experience, it is possible to become a team leader or manager. Some workers also take extra qualifications to specialise as technicians in certain fields.

Jobs and contacts

Geological technician

Assisting geologists with their work by preparing samples and providing data and other information

Technicians carry out work in the field and in the laboratory, often looking at gas, oil or minerals. They collect samples, prepare and analyse them, and produce test results from their experiments. They also evaluate their test report data and create written reports and maps of their findings.

Pros and cons
- o You usually have a standard working week, perhaps with a few extra hours at busy times.

- You will often work in a lab and wear protective clothing.
- Work requires concentrated attention for long periods.

You
- Methodical, with good attention to detail.
- Understand health and safety issues.
- An enquiring mind.
- Able to work with graphics and technical equipment.

Entry/learning
- Many employers ask for four GCSEs or S grades, with grades A*–C/1–3, including Maths and a science.
- Some employers ask for A levels or equivalent.
- Once working, you are often encouraged to study part time for NVQs/SVQs, an HND or a degree.

Money
Starting salaries are around £18,500 per year and upwards.

Career progress
You could become a senior technician and manage a team, earning £25,000–£40,000+ per year. Some people do advanced study to become geologists.

British Geological Survey www.bgs.ac.uk
Cogent Sector Skills Council Limited www.cogent-ssc.com

Laboratory technician Ⓐ

Helping scientists and technologists by performing technical support functions and running routine scientific tests

The work includes running tests on different substances, recording detailed information, and setting up, dismantling and cleaning the test equipment.

There are many different employers, including local and national government, universities, industrial companies, forensic science laboratories and hospitals.

Pros and cons
- You usually have a standard working week, but some jobs might have extra hours or shifts.
- Some tests take a long time to run, or can be repetitive.
- You can be in regular contact with dangerous chemicals or other harmful substances.

You

- Understand how to keep working areas safe, sterile and tidy.
- Good at setting up and handling lab equipment.
- Patient and accurate, with good attention to detail.
- Good communication and IT skills.

Entry/learning

- Employers tend to ask for at least four GCSEs/S grades (A–C/1–3) or equivalent, including English, Maths and a science.
- Some jobs require A levels or equivalent, or BTECs/SQAs, or higher level qualifications.
- Apprenticeships are available.

Money

Starting salaries are from £11,000 to £13,000 per year.

Career progress

There are many opportunities to specialise, or you can become a team leader or laboratory manager earning £30,000–£40,000+ per year.

**Sector Skills Council for Science, Engineering and Manufacturing Technologies www.semta.org.uk
scenta www.scenta.co.uk**

Other sectors to consider

- Engineering, manufacturing and production (see pp. 85–100)
- Healthcare (see pp. 113–118).

Family 18

Security and the armed forces

....

This work family employs around 800,000 people in the UK. Around half a million of them work in private security, 140,000 work for the police force, and about 170,000 are employed by the armed forces. Other jobs include fire and rescue services. The jobs in this field are all about protecting people, property and even countries.

Some jobs involve face-to-face contact and others are office based, supporting roles. The work can also involve shifts, long hours, potentially dangerous situations, and sometimes overseas travel. A good level of physical fitness, self-confidence and the ability to work well in a team are needed for most of these jobs.

Most work in security and the armed forces has well-defined structures for promotion and career progression. Entry to many of these jobs is via apprenticeships or cadetships.

Jobs and contacts

Coastguard watch assistant

Providing administration support to Maritime and Coastguard Agency search and rescue service teams

The work involves giving information to the general public, operating the telephones, and keeping records of all calls and rescues. Assistants also have to monitor equipment and communicate with rescuers so that they can travel to the right location.

Pros and cons
- Most work is in the operations centre (not search and rescue).
- Most work tends to be shift work, some part-time work is available.
- Emergency situations can put the whole team under pressure.
- Dealing in matters of life or death can be very upsetting.

You
- Alert and observant, and show initiative.
- Good eyesight, strong voice and hearing.
- Communication, IT and teamwork skills.
- Interest in the sea and maritime matters.

Entry/learning
- There are no set entry requirements, but Maths and English GCSEs and key skills in communication and numeracy are useful.
- Having a driving licence, previous volunteering experience and sea-going skills is very helpful.
- Training is mainly on the job, with some time spent at a training centre.

Money
Starting salaries are around £17,000 per year.

Career progress
Some coastguard watch assistants progress to watch officer level, involved in all areas of the work including searches and rescues, earning up to £24,000 per year. Overtime, allowances, and very senior/management status can bring earnings of £50,000+ per year.

Maritime and Coastguard Agency www.mcga.gov.uk
SeaVision UK www.seavisionuk.org

Door supervisor/bouncer

Helping to control people entering and leaving a building

Door supervisors stand outside buildings such as bars and nightclubs, and control any conflict situations, and the flow of people entering and leaving. They have to decide who is allowed in, and might perform searches of clothing or bags. Some door staff collect tickets, or check names on guest lists.

Pros and cons
- You are exposed to all kinds of weather conditions.
- You might need to work at unsocial hours.
- Some customers might be aggressive or might be carrying banned items.
- There might be opportunities for promotion.

You
- Aged 18 or over and physically fit.
- Calm under provocation and stress.

- o Welcoming but also assertive and understand relevant laws.
- o Excellent teamwork and communication skills.

Entry/learning
- o There are no formal entry requirements, but you must be over 18 and pass a police check.
- o If you don't have the relevant qualifications, you will start work as a trainee.
- o Trainees are expected to take a Security Industry Authority approved Level 2 course in door supervision.
- o Once qualified you gain your Door Supervision Licence, which must be renewed every three years.

Money
Trainees can earn around £13,000 per year.

Career progress
With experience, you can earn up to £18,000–£28,000 per year. Some move into other roles in the security industry, including working as guards.

Security Industry Authority www.sia.homeoffice.gov.uk

Firefighter Ⓐ

Tackling a range of emergency situations, including fires, and raising related public safety awareness

Emergency work can involve putting out fires and rescuing people from burning buildings, but it can also include rescuing people who are trapped in cars after road accidents, or affected by rail or air crashes, or trapped in lifts. The work also involves giving advice to organisations and individuals about fire safety. Regional fire services are the main employers, but this work is also offered by airports and the armed forces.

Pros and cons
- o You mostly work in shifts, based in a station, and go out when incidents occur.
- o Uniforms and protective clothing must be worn.
- o Health and safety procedures must be followed exactly.
- o The working conditions are often unpleasant and dangerous.

You
- o Physically very fit and healthy.
- o Excellent eyesight and colour vision.
- o Good team worker and trustworthy.
- o Calm under pressure with a mature attitude.

Entry/learning

- o There are no set entry requirements but some fire brigades might ask for specific GCSEs, A levels or equivalent qualifications; a clean driving licence is helpful.
- o Apprenticeships are available.
- o You must pass physicals and a number of psychological and practical tests.
- o Training is mainly on the job or on short courses from the employer.

Money

Trainees start on around £21,000 per year.

Career progress

More experienced firefighters can become trainers, supervisors or station managers, earning £22,000–£40,000 per year.

Fire Service Recruitment Information www.fireservice.co.uk

Parking attendant

Enforcing local parking areas, checking vehicles are legally parked, and issuing parking fines

Parking attendants mainly work for a local authority or a contractor firm, patrolling the nearby streets and checking for illegal parking. You sometimes need to attend court or make arrangements for cars to be clamped or towed away, or notify the police about abandoned vehicles.

Pros and cons

- o You usually work in shifts, including some weekend work.
- o The work involves lots of walking, and you will be outdoors in all weather conditions.
- o You will need to wear a uniform.
- o Some people can get aggressive when given a ticket.

You

- o Physically fit and reliable.
- o Polite but firm.
- o Understand parking regulations and the law.
- o Able to work unsupervised.

Entry/learning

- o There are no set entry requirements, but GCSEs in Maths and English can be helpful.
- o Previous experience in dealing with the public is an advantage.
- o Training is given on the job, including understanding parking laws.

o Many people study part time once in work to gain Level 2 NVQs or City & Guilds certificates.

Money
Starting salaries are around £13,000 per year.

Career progress
It is possible to become a senior attendant, and progress into supervisory or management roles. Earnings can be up to £30,000 per year.

British Parking Association www.britishparking.co.uk

Police officer

Working in a team to prevent and investigate crime, make communities safer and maintain law and order

Police officers regularly go out on patrol, and respond to emergency and other calls, dealing with accidents, assaults, robberies and other incidents, and making arrests. They also keep order at public events, and work with community groups. Other duties include keeping records, interviewing witnesses, taking statements, writing reports and giving evidence to courts.

Pros and cons
o You usually work in shifts, based at a police station or out on patrol.
o There is a chance to help people and make a difference to your community.
o Uniforms must be worn and regulations must be followed.
o You might need to deal with injured, distressed, confused or aggressive people.

You
o Good at dealing with many different types of people and honest.
o Understand the law and personal safety issues.
o Good problem-solving skills, common sense and observant.
o Physically fit and mentally robust, able to work well under pressure.

Entry/learning
o No specific qualifications are needed, but you must be over 17 and a half years old to apply.
o A medical and several other tests must be passed, including eyesight and written tests, and a criminal records check.
o Once accepted, new recruits undergo two years of training on the Initial Police Learning and Development Programme, which includes classroom learning and practical experience.

Money

The starting salary for a student police officer is around £22,000 per year.

Career progress

Once trained, police officers can specialise and train for different departments, and it is also possible to move upwards to the level of sergeant and inspector. Salaries can be from £24,000–£60,000+ per year.

Police Service Recruitment www.policecouldyou.co.uk

Prison officer

Supervising criminals who have been sentenced to time in prison

Officers are responsible for keeping prisoners securely in prison, and, where possible, help them to become law-abiding people when their sentence ends. Most work is indoors in a secure environment. Duties include supervising everyday activities, escorting inmates to and from court, working with visitors, writing reports and carrying out security checks and searches.

Pros and cons

- o The work is mainly on a shift basis, including nights and weekends.
- o Uniforms must be worn and safety procedures followed.
- o Helping people to rehabilitate themselves can be rewarding.
- o You might need to deal with difficult and violent prisoners.

You

- o Physically fit, confident and calm.
- o Excellent communication skills.
- o Understand and respect prisoners' rights.
- o Tactful but assertive when needed.

Entry/learning

- o Entry requirements vary, but no specific academic qualifications are usually needed.
- o Applicants must pass a medical, an eyesight test, a background check and a fitness test.
- o Work begins with an eight-week training course, and other training is done on the job.

Money

Starting salaries in England and Wales are around £18,000 per year.

Career progress

It is possible to be promoted to senior officer level and above, earning £29,000–£31,000 per year.

Skills for Justice www.skillsforjustice.com

RAF airman/woman

Working in several specialised roles to support the peacekeeping, transportation and defence needs of the Royal Air Force (RAF)

Airmen and airwomen make up the majority of people employed by the RAF. After basic fitness, weapons and aircraft training, you specialise for different roles. These include engineering and technical work, force protection, medical and administrative work, air operations support such as radar monitoring, communications and catering.

Pros and cons
- You usually have a standard working week, but must always be available for duty in case of emergency.
- You are mainly stationed at RAF bases, but sometimes posted overseas.
- You can be away from friends and family for long periods.
- You might be working in very dangerous and stressful situations.

You
- Loyal, self-disciplined and able to follow orders.
- High level of physical fitness.
- Work well in a team and remain calm under pressure.
- Attention to detail and good at analysing information.

Entry/learning
- Entry requirements vary according to the specialist role, from no formal qualifications to two A levels.
- You must be aged 16 or over to apply.
- You must pass a medical, a fitness test, interviews and written tests.
- If accepted, you must attend training courses at RAF Halton in Buckinghamshire and RAF College Cranwell in Lincolnshire, followed by specialised training in your chosen role.

Money
Initial salary is around £13,500 per year during early training.

Career progress
After completing specialist training, recruits are promoted to the post of leading aircraftman/aircraftwoman, earning around £16,000 per year. There are further opportunities to train,

specialise and be promoted through the ranks, with sergeants earning up to £36,000 per year.

Royal Air Force Careers www.raf.mod.uk

Interview

Chris, RAF Airman,
age 18

'I joined the RAF basically for a challenge, a *big* new challenge, and because it's not the usual office based nine-to-five. I wanted somewhere with new experiences and real chances to progress. And I want to serve my country, I know it sounds corny to some but it does mean a lot to me to put on that uniform and be part of an elite unit.

'They don't just take anybody, it's hard to get in, they pick and choose the best. I had an interview and a medical and a BFT (basic fitness test), and you have this aptitude test too that's designed to guide them on the best trade you could go into. I'm working in FP (Force Protection) now, in regiment, where you're the soldiering side of the RAF working outside the base perimeter. The next step for me will be passing the trade ability tests to become a Senior Aircraftman.'

Royal Navy rating

Protecting the UK's ports and coastline, and undertaking international missions, including humanitarian work and combat

Ratings work on naval bases, and on board ships and submarines. They are responsible for operating, maintaining and repairing technical equipment, and each specialises in one of six main trades: warfare, engineering, logistics, medical, fleet air, and submarine.

Pros and cons
o You will be working on some weekends and public holidays, and be on call in case of emergencies.
o You will be living on board ships and submarines, or at an onshore naval station.
o The working conditions can sometimes be dangerous and stressful.
o You can be posted abroad on short notice.

You

- Work well in a team and follow orders.
- Solve problems and react quickly under stress.
- Excellent level of physical fitness and able to swim.
- Able to live and work at close quarters with many others.

Entry/learning

- There are usually no entry requirements, apart from a few trades.
- You must be at least 16 years of age on entry.
- You will have to pass a medical test, a fitness test, and other written and verbal tests.
- New recruits undergo nine weeks of basic training, followed by specialist training in their chosen trade.

Money

Starting salary is around £13,500 per year. Recruits tend to pay very low amounts for rent and for Council Tax, as these are usually subsidised by the employer.

Career progress

After initial training there are opportunities to progress though the Navy's promotion structure up to the level of leading rating, earning around £16,000–£32,500, depending on trade and rank.

The Royal Navy www.royalnavy.mod.uk

Security officer/guard Ⓐ

Protecting people, places, property or money

Security officers monitor and patrol the organisations and buildings they are assigned to protect, or they might protect people and valuable items on the move. Most security officers use security systems, monitoring devices and other technology. Some of the work involves driving security vans and collecting money safely.

Pros and cons

- You often have to do shift work or work in unsocial hours.
- You might be indoors or you might have to be outdoors, regardless of weather conditions.
- There is an opportunity to work with new technology and equipment.
- You will need to wear a uniform or protective clothing.

You

- Reliable, polite, responsible and honest.
- Respond quickly in a crisis.

- Good level of fitness.
- Able to use IT and surveillance equipment and write reports.

Entry/learning
- You must be aged 18 or over and agree to a criminal records check; a driving licence is useful.
- Before you can work, you must gain an industry licence approved by the Security Industry Authority – this is an assessment delivered over four days and you have to pay for it.
- Apprenticeships might be available.
- Some employers offer extra training, such as Level 2 NVQs in providing security services, and there are higher qualifications available after that.

Money
Starting salaries range from £13,000 to £20,000 per year.

Career progress
With training and experience it is possible to become a site manager or area manager, earning £26,000 to £50,000+ per year.

Skills for Security www.skillsforsecurity.org.uk
Security Industry Authority www.sia.homeoffice.gov.uk

Soldier

Defending the UK and its allies around the world, and participating in peacekeeping and humanitarian operations

Soldiers are trained to be physically fit and ready for combat. Soldiers also specialise and train for one of over 130 jobs, including engineering, intelligence, communications, medical and musical. Those over 18 years old can apply to join their choice of army regiment.

Pros and cons
- You might have a standard working week or work in shifts, according to the type of job, and you will be on call for emergencies.
- Sometimes you are posted abroad at short notice, although this can be seen as an opportunity to travel the world.
- You will spend long periods apart from friends and loved ones.
- You might be working in very dangerous situations, under a lot of stress.
- You might feel it is an honour to represent and defend your country.

You
- Self-disciplined, loyal and able to follow orders.
- Excellent team worker and responsible.

o Calm under stress and able to act on your own initiative.
o Physically fit and practical.

Entry/learning
o No formal qualifications are required for some jobs, but others need specific GCSEs or equivalent.
o Apprenticeships are available for some jobs.
o You must be aged 16 or over to sign up, and pass the Army Entrance Test, a medical test, a fitness test and an interview.
o All recruits first undergo phase 1 and phase 2 training, and then begin specialist training for their chosen job.

Money
New recruits earn around £13,500 per year.

Career progress
There is a well-defined career structure. After initial training, qualified privates earn around £16,500–£25,500 per year, and the highest-ranking soldiers can earn over £45,000 per year.

Army Jobs www.armyjobs.mod.uk

Other jobs to consider

o Ministry of Defence police officer

o Police community support officer

o Police support worker **A**

o Trainee RAF officer

o Royal Marines commando

o Security systems installer **A**

o Store detective.

Family 19

Social work and counselling services

All the jobs in this family are about helping other people, sometimes when they are under stress or having problems. They include counselling and therapy jobs, social care and support work, advice services and charity jobs. Employers include the NHS, local authorities, private organisations, and charities and non-profit groups.

Staff in this field need very good interpersonal skills, emotional maturity and a kind personality. They also need to be good listeners, and have observation skills. Some employers ask for specific qualifications or previous experience for certain roles, but there are many other jobs that don't have particular entry requirements or that can be started via an apprenticeship.

Working for a large employer usually means that there are opportunities to take on extra responsibilities and gain promotion. Many employers encourage continuing professional development, and extra study can allow workers to specialise in other forms of work or become fully qualified in their chosen field.

Jobs and contacts

Childminder

Looking after children, mainly in your own home

Childminding includes feeding, changing, bathing and dressing younger children, and preparing meals for older children. It also includes planning and running fun and learning activities for them, including games and creative play. Some childminders supervise children on trips, or take them to and from playgroup or school.

Pros and cons
- Working from home can suit people who have children of their own.
- Working with children can be rewarding and fun.

- o The hours can be long and some tasks are unpleasant.
- o The work might involve lots of lifting and carrying.

You
- o Patient, imaginative and caring.
- o Good communication and observation skills.
- o Awareness of health and safety issues, with a safe home.
- o Fit and energetic.

Entry/learning
- o No academic qualifications are needed, but qualifications in childcare are useful.
- o Childminders must be at least 18 years old and registered with Ofsted (Office for Standards in Education) before they can care for children under 8 years of age.
- o You can study part time or by distance learning to gain a range of qualifications such as Level 3 certificates from the Council for Awards in Children's Education, the National Childminding Association, the Scottish Childminding Association, or the Northern Ireland Childminding Association.

Money
Most childminders are self-employed and charge an hourly rate of £3–£6.50 per hour for each child. Full-timers can earn around £9,500 per year when starting out, but this depends on the number of children.

Career progress
Some childminders become network coordinators, trainers, or care assistants, or qualify to work as nursery nurses. With experience, you can earn £13,000–£25,000 per year.

Office for Standards in Education www.ofsted.gov.uk
National Childminding Association of England and Wales www.ncma.org.uk

---

Social care worker

Giving practical and emotional support to vulnerable people

This job involves helping vulnerable people, such as people with mental health problems or learning difficulties, with the challenges of everyday life. This might include washing, shopping, eating or going on outings. Employers include local authorities, private care homes, the NHS, charities and daycare centres.

Pros and cons
- o You usually have a standard working week, but some jobs are live-in and involve staying in a person's home or a care facility.

- Helping people can be very rewarding.
- The work is sometimes physically or emotionally challenging.

You

- Approachable, caring and patient.
- Good at keeping records.
- Sensitive to needs for privacy and dignity.
- Practical and persistent.

Entry/learning

- There are no set entry requirements for many jobs, but volunteer or work experience can be very useful.
- Most training is on the job, or employers might send workers on short courses.
- Many care workers are encouraged to study part time to gain vocational qualifications such as NVQs/SVQs.

Money

Starting salaries are around £11,000 per year, with less for apprentices.

Career progress

With experience and qualifications, some care workers become supervisors or coordinators with salaries up to £28,000 per year.

Skills for Care www.skillsforcare.org.uk

Other jobs to consider

- Community development worker **A**

Family 20

Transport and logistics

Transport and logistics are all about moving people or goods around by road, rail, air or sea, both within the UK and abroad. Jobs in this family are varied, and fall into several different categories, such as:

- delivery services
- driving and moving goods
- importing and exporting
- maintenance
- passenger care/customer service.

Lots of these jobs need driving licences or other skills and certificates, and many of them involve working with the public, so customer service skills are often needed too. Sometimes the work can be fast paced, and an ability to stay calm and work well under pressure can be very helpful.

There are plenty of opportunities for school leavers, with a range of entry-level jobs and many different apprenticeships to consider, although some work has age restrictions. Larger employers often have their own training schemes as well.

Jobs and contacts

Postman/postwoman

Collecting, sorting and delivering mail to homes, businesses and other organisations

Staff sort and pack mail ready for delivery on their route, and set out on foot, or by bicycle or van, to deliver it. They might be responsible for collecting mail from post boxes or nearby places of work. They also have to get signatures for items of registered post.

Pros and cons

- o Work starts early in the morning, around 5a.m., might have shifts.
- o Lots of time is spent outdoors in all weathers.
- o Some rounds have regular hazards on them.
- o The work involves much standing, walking, cycling or driving.

You

- o Reliable, responsible and trustworthy.
- o Physically fit and able to walk long distances.
- o Good customer service skills.
- o Like being outside a lot.

Entry/learning

- o There are no set entry requirements for this job, but you must pass an aptitude test (to make sure you can read well), a fitness test, an interview and a medical test.
- o Some apprenticeships are available, and you might be able to start at age 16 – non-apprentices must be 18 or over.
- o A full driving licence or cycling ability can be very helpful.
- o On-the-job training lasts for 18 months, and you are encouraged to work towards the Level 2 NVQ/SVQ in Mail Services.

Money

Starting salaries are around £13,500–£15,500 per year, with less for apprentices.

Career progress

After training and one year of practical experience, it is possible to start training for supervisory or management work, earning £18,500–£28,000 per year. Some people move into sales, marketing, or parcel deliveries.

Royal Mail Group plc www.royalmail.com
Skills for Logistics www.skillsforlogistics.org

Trainee road transport manager

Planning the routes and timetables of your employer's vehicles, and monitoring their progress

Road transport managers plan timetables, journeys and loads to move passengers or goods around. They are also responsible for putting health and safety regulations into place, checking on vehicle progress and dealing with suppliers, breakdowns and customer complaints.

Pros and cons

- Some businesses work 24 hours per day, so you might need to work weekends or shifts.
- Work is mainly in an office, with some depot visits.
- Every day is different and varied.
- There will be opportunities for promotion in many organisations.

You

- Organised, analytical and logical.
- Good interpersonal and motivational skills.
- Work well under pressure and to tight deadlines.
- An interest in IT and road transport.

Entry/learning

- Some businesses ask for five or more GCSEs (A*–C) or equivalent plus two A levels, others will ask for a degree or equivalent.
- Apprenticeships might be available.
- Once working, you can study part time for Chartered Institute of Logistics and Transport professional qualifications.
- Further qualifications are needed to progress to senior management positions.

Money

Starting salaries are around £15,000–£23,000 per year.

Career progress

With extra qualifications it is possible to move into more senior management, earning £25,000–£65,000 per year.

Chartered Institute of Logistics and Transport www.ciltuk.org.uk
Skills for Logistics www.skillsforlogistics.org

Trainee bus/coach driver

Providing a scheduled transport service for passengers making long or short journeys

Bus drivers pick up and drop off passengers at agreed times and places, according to a schedule or timetable. They help passengers on board, and ensure their safety and comfort during the journey. Some drivers also check or sell tickets and travel passes.

Pros and cons

- Usually the work is in shifts, which might include evenings, nights or weekends.
- You might be working away from home for some jobs.

o Some passengers can be difficult or abusive, but others are grateful and it can be rewarding to keep part of the transport system running smoothly.

o Long journeys can become tiring or repetitive, but many drivers enjoy the opportunity to get out on the road and work with large vehicles.

You

o Good eyesight and concentration.

o Excellent driving ability and understand and follow laws.

o Good customer service skills, polite and assertive.

o Able to stick to a strict timetable.

Entry/learning

o You must be aged 18 or over; some work requires you to be at least 21.

o You must hold a Passenger Carrying Vehicle (PCV) licence and a Driver Certificate of Professional Competence (Driver CPC).

o Some employers will take you on as a trainee at age 18, and fund you while you take your PCV licence – there are no specific academic requirements but employers might ask for four GCSEs (A–C) or equivalent, including English and Maths.

o Once working, you can study part time for a Level 2 NVQ in Passenger Carrying Vehicle Driving.

Money

Trainees earn around £11,000 per year.

Career progress

Once qualified it is possible to earn £16,000–£23,500 per year. Some move into trainer or management roles.

Go Skills www.careersinpassengertransport.org
Driving Standards Agency www.dsa.gov.uk

Trainee large goods vehicle (LGV) driver

Distributing goods around the UK and mainland Europe in a large goods vehicle

LGV drivers collect, transport and deliver many different kinds of goods. They work with transport managers to plan their routes, and load and unload their vehicle contents safely. Drivers are also responsible for routine vehicle maintenance checks, and ensuring delivery paperwork is filled out.

Pros and cons

o Part-time work and flexible working hours are possible, or you might be working shifts.

- You might need to be away from home for days.
- Driving alone can become lonely or monotonous.

You
- Able to work well alone.
- Excellent driving skills, reaction speed and eyesight.
- Polite when dealing with customers.
- Good at sticking to schedules.

Entry/learning
- No specific academic qualifications are needed, but drivers must be over 21 and hold a LGV licence and a Driver Certificate of Professional Competence (Driver CPC).
- School leavers aged 16 and over can apply for traineeships from Skills for Logistics (see below).
- Apprenticeships are also available for those aged 16–24.

Money
When just starting out you can earn £9,000–£14,000 per year.

Career progress
With experience, or working in a specialist field, you can earn £24,000–£36,000 per year. Some drivers set up their own businesses.

Skills for Logistics www.skillsforlogistics.org
Driving Standards Agency www.dsa.gov.uk

Interview

Andrew, LGV Driver,
age 21

'Companies (usually) want you to have both an LGV licence and some driving experience. The next village from us is a close-knit community and I was lucky – the family haulage firm there knew some of my relatives and they took me on as a trainee so I started with no experience. I got my LGV licence as quickly as I could. I always wanted to travel and go all over Europe to see real life in those countries, and that was the main reason to get the licence. I had a fantastic time on my first trip, amazing scenery, crossing the French Alps.

'There are rules about when you can drive and how long for. All the trucks have tachographs and you have your ID card and you feed it into these machines and input your hours and type of work into it. You can work a maximum of 40 hours per week, you must have 11 hours off every day, and do no more than four and a half hours' driving at a stretch. It all gets very complicated, we have huge booklets on it, and the rules keep changing and getting tweaked.'

Other jobs to consider

- ○ Airport baggage handler
- ○ Courier Ⓐ
- ○ Lift truck operator Ⓐ
- ○ Loader
- ○ Port operative ⊗ Ⓐ
- ○ Rail control room operator Ⓐ
- ○ Rail signalling technician Ⓐ
- ○ Removals operative
- ○ Taxi driver
- ○ Train driver Ⓐ
- ○ Van driver Ⓐ
- ○ Vehicle removal technician Ⓐ
- ○ Warehouse worker Ⓐ.

Import/export clerk

Providing administrative support to companies that source or sell their goods overseas

Import/export clerks complete all the necessary paperwork or online documentation needed for selling, buying and transporting goods. They might also liaise with transport companies (air, sea, rail or road) or specialist freight forwarders to get the best prices, and keep records of costings and transactions.

197

Pros and cons
- You might have a standard working week, or work different hours to suit non-UK time zones.
- There is a chance to learn and use many skills.
- If you are promoted there will be opportunities for overseas travel.
- Working conditions are sometimes pressured and stressful.

You
- Excellent communication skills.
- Good with numbers and IT.
- Accurate and methodical.
- Work well under pressure and keep to deadlines.

Entry/learning
- There are no set qualification requirements, but employers usually ask for at least four GCSEs (A*–C) or equivalent, and some ask for A levels or degrees.
- It is common to start as a trainee in a junior administration position; apprenticeships are also available for those aged 16–24.
- Training is on the job.
- Once trained, there are many opportunities to gain professional qualifications from the Institute of Export and other organisations.

Money
Trainees tend to start on annual salaries of around £11,000–£16,000 per year.

Career progress
It is possible to progress to team leader or import/export manager, or to move into sales positions, earning £30,000–£65,000+ per year.

Institute of Export www.export.org.uk
Skills for Logistics www.skillsforlogistics.org

Other jobs to consider
- Freight forwarder
- Merchant navy rating
- Purchasing clerk **A**.

Rail track maintenance operative

Building, inspecting, maintaining and repairing the rail track network

Rail track maintenance operatives work on railway tracks and also on the nearby railway embankments, fencing and bridges. They lay and replace sections of track, and use a variety of tools and heavy machinery. They are also responsible for inspecting the track for potential faults. Network Rail is the main employer.

Pros and cons
- The work is often done at night to minimise disruption to the train timetable.
- The work is mainly outdoors in all weather conditions.
- It can be rewarding to see the results of your work.
- The work is physically very demanding.

You
- Physically fit and strong, with excellent hearing and normal colour vision.
- Good manual skills for working with tools.
- Work well in a team.
- Responsible and respect health and safety practices.

Entry/learning
- You will usually be asked for at least four GCSEs (A–C) or equivalent, including English, Maths and perhaps a science or Design and Technology.
- Employers might ask you to undergo a medical test, a fitness test, hearing and eyesight tests, and a criminal records check.
- Apprenticeships are available for those aged 16–24.
- Once accepted, you will attend the employer's training course, followed by on-the-job training.

Money
Starting salaries are around £14,000 per year.

Career progress
With experience and perhaps supervisory responsibilities, it is possible to earn £18,000–£25,000 per year. Some people become technical specialists, or train as managers or engineers.

Network Rail www.networkrail.co.uk

> ## Other jobs to consider
>
> ○ Airfield maintenance worker **A**.

Air cabin crew

Welcoming passengers and making sure they have a safe, comfortable journey

Cabin crew check the cabin before welcoming the passengers on board, and prepare them for their flight with safety procedures and information. Once in the air they provide food and drinks, sell gift items, and deal with any in-flight questions or other issues. They then prepare the passengers and cabin for a safe landing and see passengers off the plane.

Pros and cons
- ○ The working hours are usually long, with shifts and weekend work.
- ○ You get an opportunity to travel the world and meet new people.
- ○ You work in cramped and noisy conditions, and are responsible for keeping work areas clean and organised.
- ○ There is a risk of emergencies occurring on flights.

You
- ○ Friendly, approachable and able to give clear instructions.
- ○ Well groomed, confident and assertive.
- ○ Calm under pressure and reassuring.
- ○ Good team worker who is efficient and organised.

Entry/learning
- ○ Entry requirements vary, but employers might ask for four or more GCSEs (A–C) or equivalent, and entrants must be aged 18 or over and physically fit.
- ○ There are height and weight restrictions, you must be able to swim, and having a second or third language is a big advantage.
- ○ Training is on employer-run courses and on the job.
- ○ Level 2 NVQs and other industry-related qualifications are also available, including City & Guilds, EMTA Awards Limited, NCFE and Ascentis.

Money
Starting salaries are around £12,000–£14,500 per year.

Career progress
Possible to progress to the roles of purser, senior cabin crew, supervisor or cabin services director, earning £18,000–£25,000+ per year.

Go Skills www.careersinpassengertransport.org

Passenger transport clerk

Selling tickets for coach or rail travel, and dealing with general customer enquiries

This is a customer service role dealing with rail or coach passenger enquiries about departure times, fares, delays, routes and connections. Clerks are also responsible for selling or refunding tickets. Employers include bus and coach operators, rail companies, the London Underground and Eurostar.

Pros and cons
- You might have a standard working week, or be working shifts, including evenings and weekends.
- You might be based at a station or at a customer contact/call centre.
- The work can sometimes be repetitive or pressured.
- Some customers can be frustrated or confrontational.

You
- Friendly, polite, efficient and helpful.
- Good maths and IT skills, and a good memory.
- Clear speaking voice and a good telephone manner.
- Work well under pressure and patient.

Entry/learning
- No formal qualifications are required, but you are likely to be asked for GCSEs or equivalent in English and Maths, and key skills in IT are useful.
- Customer service experience is an advantage.
- Apprenticeships might be available for railway work.
- Most training is on courses from the employer, and on the job, and you might also wish to study part time for customer service-related NVQs.

Money
Starting salaries are around £13,500–£14,500 per year.

Career progress
With experience and qualifications it is possible to progress to supervisory or management roles, earning £17,000–£20,000+ per year.

Go Skills www.careersinpassengertransport.org

Train conductor

Working on trains to check and issue tickets and provide general customer assistance

Conductors work on board a train making sure passengers are safe and comfortable, checking and selling tickets, and responding to passenger queries and complaints. They also make passenger announcements using the train's public address system, operate the doors and help passengers get on and off safely, and report and deal with any on-train incidents.

Pros and cons
- Working hours are usually a shift pattern, with some evening and weekend hours.
- A uniform must be worn when on duty.
- You sometimes have to deal with difficult situations or passengers.
- You work with a variety of different people.

You
- Excellent customer service skills.
- Confident working alone.
- Calm, quick and reliable under pressure.
- Physically fit, with good eyesight and hearing.

Entry/learning
- There are no set qualifications but most train operating companies ask for GCSEs in English and Maths, and previous customer service experience is an advantage.
- The usual entry age is 18, but you can gain entry at 16 via apprenticeships or company trainee schemes.
- You must pass medical and fitness tests, sight, colour vision and hearing tests, a criminal records check, and often also drug and alcohol tests.
- Employers offer initial training courses, followed by on-the-job training and it is possible to study part time for Level 2 NVQs and other qualifications.

Money
Starting salaries are around £12,500–£16,000 per year.

Career progress
Experienced conductors can earn £14,000–£20,000 per year and many move into supervisory or train manager roles.

Go Skills www.careersinpassengertransport.org

Other jobs to consider

o Cruise ship steward

o Passenger check-in officer

o Railway station assistant **Ⓐ**.

Part 3

The Toolkit
(or Resources)

If you've been offered your first full-time job, an apprenticeship or other trainee post, then congratulations. It's an exciting time in your life, and it can also be quite a daunting experience because there's so much to learn. In this final part of the book, Chapter 6 will guide you through the first days and months of your career, and Chapter 7 recommends a range of further resources to give you all the best help and information you might need.

Chapter 6
Your brilliant career

F rom the moment you're offered your first employment or training contract, your life starts to change. If you want to hit the ground running with your new job then you will probably find some or all of these topics useful:

- ○ starting work
- ○ career development
- ○ leaving home.

Starting work
Contracts
Within two months of starting work, make sure you have been given a contract. It can be verbal or in writing, but it is your right to be given a written contract by the employer if you ask for one. Read the whole thing very carefully, and look for what the employer is offering and expecting. For example, you should check for these details:

- ○ the hours they want you to work
- ○ where you will be working
- ○ the pay they are offering
- ○ how often you will be paid
- ○ when they want you to start
- ○ whether you are a permanent employee or if there's a set time that you will be working there
- ○ whether you are classed as a full-time employee, a full-time trainee or something else
- ○ the training they officially offer
- ○ amount of holiday they allow you
- ○ overtime hours and overtime pay
- ○ sick pay and redundancy pay
- ○ how much notice they have to give if you are sacked or made redundant
- ○ how much notice you must give them if you wish to leave

- O   workplace disciplinary, dismissal and grievance procedures
- O   whether you can join the employer's pension scheme.

Some of this information might be given to you as part of other documents, such as a staff handbook or an induction pack. If there's anything you don't understand, or don't want to agree to, then it's important to get the contract checked as soon as you can. Try careers support staff at school or college, a Connexions adviser or your nearest Citizens Advice Bureau.

If you decide you are happy with the contract, sign it and return it to the employer. Make sure that you keep a copy for yourself as well.

The first day

The first day at a new job can be nerve-wracking, but if you want it to go well:

- O   turn up slightly early, with any paperwork you've been asked for
- O   remember the name of the person you're supposed to ask for on arrival
- O   take everything you think you'll need with you
- O   dress smartly for office work or working with the public, or wear the correct protective clothing if required
- O   make sure you have good personal hygiene
- O   if you don't know something, ASK
- O   do not leave early - wait until your manager or supervisor tells you it's time to leave, in case they want to catch up with you to see how you found your first day.

The most important thing to do is give the impression that you are respectful and friendly, so be polite to everyone, not just the boss. Remember to smile, make eye contact and shake hands, and be positive – don't criticise people, places or the new job. Chat politely when you meet people in social areas such as the canteen or kitchenette. Beware of 'office politics', and don't be too quick to team up with anyone or take sides.

You might find that you are not given any 'real' work on the first day while you settle in. If that's the case:

- O   spend time learning as much as you can about the organisation
- O   try to have a tour of the workplace with someone who knows it well
- O   ask your supervisor for one or two things to do
- O   don't spend ages looking bored or hanging around.

The first few weeks

You will want to get settled in, and you need to make a good impression too. Try to be as professional as you can by:

- O   offering to help with projects or smaller things
- O   always turning up on time

- asking questions when you don't understand something
- watching your colleagues to see what time most of them leave, and following their lead
- not making personal calls on the company phone, or in front of colleagues – use your breaks or lunch hour to make these calls
- keeping the noise down when you are using the phone or doing other work
- keeping your work area tidy and not leaving a mess for other people to clear up
- planning your time well, so that you can do all of the work that you've been asked to do
- not taking too many long tea breaks, cigarette breaks or toilet breaks
- being polite and friendly with everyone – try to get to know all of your colleagues.

Money matters

Your contract of employment must tell you how often you will be paid. As soon as you receive your first payment of wages, your employer must provide you with a payslip to go with them. This is a written record of how much you have been paid, and what deductions your employer has taken out of them.

The most common deductions shown on payslips are for:

- income tax
- national insurance
- pension schemes.

Anyone who is working or doing an apprenticeship must pay income tax and national insurance on their earnings.

Income tax is payable on your overall 'taxable income' during the tax year (6 April to 5 April) if it goes above a certain level. This includes your earnings from any job, jobseeker's allowance if you're claiming it, certain other benefits and any interest you get on your savings.

Everyone in the UK can have a certain amount of income without having to pay any income tax. This is called your 'personal allowance'. In the tax year 2010–11, the personal allowance for everyone under the age of 65 is £6,475 per year – meaning you won't pay any income tax on income up to that amount. If your total income for a year is above the personal allowance, you'll pay income tax on the rest. For current tax rates and a full explanation of how taxes work, see www.taxmatters.hmrc.gov.uk.

National insurance contributions are deducted from your earnings if you earn over a certain amount. They go towards your state pension and help pay for other state benefits if you're employed. If you don't keep up with your contributions, you could lose the right to other benefits, such as jobseeker's allowance or statutory payments, e.g. statutory sick pay. You also might not receive a full state pension when you retire. You need a national insurance number to work in the UK, and also to claim benefits. See www.inlandrevenue.gov.uk if you do not have one, or call 0845 600 0643.

Everyone who is working should make sure that they're getting at least the **national minimum wage**. See www.hmrc.gov.uk/nmw or ring the National Minimum Wage Helpline on 0800 917 2368 (opening hours: 8.00a.m. to 8.00p.m., Monday to Friday, 9.00a.m. to 1.00p.m., Saturday).

There are three levels of minimum wage, as follows:

- £5.93 per hour for workers aged 21 years and older
- a development rate of £4.92 per hour for workers aged 18–20 inclusive
- £3.64 per hour for all workers under the age of 18, who are no longer of compulsory school age.

Please note that:

- the rate is £2.50 per hour for apprentices under the age of 19
- the rate is £2.50 per hour for apprentices over the age of 19 and in the first 12 months
- apprentices aged 19 or over who have completed the first 12 months of their apprenticeship are entitled to the full national minimum wage rate for their age group.

Your employer might have a **pension scheme** that you can join. While retirement can seem a long way off, some pensions can be a worthwhile investment and money you save when you are young has more time to grow over the years.

Health and safety

The employer is responsible for your health and safety at work. In your first few days you should be told about:

- fire exits, fire drills and what to do if there is a fire
- who the first aid person is, and where to find the first aid kit
- anything special about your job or the workplace, such as risks, or special clothing or other protection you might need.

To find out more about staying safe at work, visit www.wiseup2work.co.uk.

Your rights

Young workers are often confused about their rights. For example, if you're working longer than four and a half hours at a time, you're entitled to a break of at least 30 minutes. The relationship between you and your employer is determined by your employment contract, so read it carefully. Spoken contracts are legally binding too (search for 'verbal contract' on www.adviceguide.org.uk to find out more). Employers are responsible for providing adequate insurance cover and training you in health and safety issues.

You also have statutory rights: all workers must be treated fairly and you should not be discriminated against because of your sex, race, any disability or trade union membership.

There are several helplines and useful websites listed on pages 221–223; use this list if you are having problems with working hours, low wages, discrimination or harassment. This official website is a helpful place to start if you are having problems at work: www. direct.gov.uk/en/Employment/ResolvingWorkplaceDisputes/DiscriminationAtWork/ index.htm.

Rights guides for young workers

Some useful, comprehensive guides to your working rights:

http://static.advicenow.org.uk/files/young-workers-2009-1587.pdf

www.worksmart.org.uk/rights/young_workers_under_18

www.unison.org.uk/acrobat/17635.pdf

Unemployment and redundancy

If you're having trouble finding a job or training, or you lose your job because of redundancy or dismissal (getting sacked), try not to panic and consider all of your options before looking for new work/training/study opportunities. You should also start to claim for any benefits or other payments that might be due to you, such as redundancy payments.

If you live in England, Wales or Scotland, contact your local Jobcentre Plus office. The Jobcentre Plus office can help you to find work or a training place, and you might also be able to make a claim for jobseeker's allowance. Alternatively you can call the freephone number 0800 055 6688 or text 0800 023 4888. The Welsh language line number is 0800 012 1888.

Your local Citizens Advice Bureau can give you free, impartial advice about your rights in general if you lose your job or training place, and can also give you advice about money problems and benefits you might be able to claim. Visit a local office, or check the website:

www.adviceguide.org.uk/index/life/benefits/young_people_and_benefits.htm.

For official government advice about your rights if being made redundant or getting dismissed, visit www.direct.gov.uk/en/Employment/index.htm.

Career development

It's rare to get a promotion shortly after starting work, but most people hope to progress in their careers after a while. This usually needs a combination of the following four aspects:

1. showing commitment and dedication to the job you currently have
2. offering to take on new responsibilities, or accepting them when they are offered

3. doing extra study and qualifications

4. having a long-term goal or a plan.

Extra study and qualifications

Apprenticeships and trainee posts should lead to recognised qualifications, but if your job doesn't offer this, then consider doing some extra study or training to improve your career prospects. You can:

o   take evening classes in a range of subjects. Visit www.learndirect.co.uk to find out what some of your options are

o   try distance learning schemes, where you study in the evening or at weekends,

o   try to persuade your employer to offer, or pay for, some recognised training

o   if you are aged 16 or 17 and did not get any Level 2 qualifications at school you could get Time Off for Study or Training (TfST). See www.connexions-direct. com for more details.

Leaving home

You might have to move to another town to get the job that you want, or you might just feel that it's time to get your own place. The two most important things to get right are your accommodation and your finances.

If you aren't already used to doing your own laundry, cooking or cleaning, these are all useful skills to learn before you leave home. Parents or legal guardians will help you out if you ask them for advice about things such as laundry, but if in doubt read the instructions inside the clothes, on the front of the washing machine or the laundry detergent packet.

You don't have to be the next celebrity chef when it comes to food either, just get together a handful of simple recipes that don't need too many pans or gadgets. To get started in the kitchen, buy simple cookbooks such as *The Complete Cookery Course* by Delia Smith (BBC Consumer Publishing, £9.99), or *The Essential Student Cookbook* by Cas Clarke (Hodder Headline, £5.99), or try searching one of the BBC food websites.

Staying healthy in a new town

o   It's a good idea to register with a local GP as soon as you move house, just in case.

o   NHS Direct: this advice helpline (0845 46 47; calls taken 24 hours daily) is staffed by trained NHS nurses, plus there is a website containing comprehensive, easy to understand advice (www.nhsdirect.nhs.uk).

o   Netdoctor.co.uk: the UK's leading independent health website, with drug and illness encyclopaedias, message boards and an email query service.

Housing

Unless you're prepared to become a lodger or rent a bedsit, you'll probably end up in a shared house because that is the cheapest housing option. If you're moving to a new town you will have to travel to the area and view properties, preferably with a friend or relative for safety, or book a temporary room, then house hunt during your first few days in town. Meet the other tenants before you sign anything, as you could end up sharing with anyone. Be prepared to look around for a while to find somewhere suitable.

Follow these safety tips when looking at accommodation:

- never go there alone, always go with someone else
- go during daylight hours
- tell someone exactly where you're going and when you'll be back
- if you get a bad feeling, trust your instincts and leave.

Questions to ask.

- How much is the monthly rent and the deposit?
- Do they provide pans, kettles, crockery, cutlery, furniture, laundry facilities, broadband internet access and telephone points?
- What are the kitchen and bathroom facilities, type of heating and hot water supply?
- If you're bringing a car ask about parking places and parking permits.
- Find out what other bills you pay on top of your rent, their average costs, and how often they are due.

Important things to look for:

- the distance from shops and the public transport timetable
- parking spaces or bike storage
- the feel of the local area: safe at night, nice neighbours?
- look at everything (each room, inside cupboards, roof tiles, back of house)
- the size of the bedroom
- strong front and back doors and gates with decent locks, secure windows
- signs of damp or mildew, such as a musty smell or black spores
- draughty doors, cracked windows
- infestations: mouse droppings, slime trails, dead insects
- safety certificates for all gas appliances, carbon monoxide detectors
- state of electrical wiring and appliances
- easy exit in case of fire; smoke alarms, fire extinguishers
- state of repair of the kitchen and bathroom
- what's in the kitchen: crockery, pans and cutlery, freezer, washing machine?
- general state of furniture, mattresses, carpets, etc.
- telephone landline and sockets.

Signing a housing contract

Once you've found the right place, you need to sign a contract and pay a deposit. The contract is legally binding so read the small print before signing it. If anything seems unreasonable or confusing, get it checked by your local Citizens Advice Bureau. Your contract will probably be an 'assured shorthold tenancy', lasting for at least six months. Check whether it's a single or joint tenancy agreement. With single tenancy each person is only liable for their share of rent and bills, but joint tenancy means that if one of you defaults on the rent, the rest of you can be charged.

Check the following:

- start and end dates of contract
- monthly rent and deposit
- charges for late rent
- landlord's responsibilities
- landlord's full contact details
- notice period.

Once you've signed the contract, you should be given your own copy before you move in. Keep it safe, in case you need to refer to it later. An oral contract is also legally binding, but hard to prove in court.

Inventory

The inventory is a list of everything in the property, and when you are given one make sure to check thoroughly around the house to see if it's correct. If you aren't shown an inventory, ask for one.

Deposit

The deposit is a sum of money, usually the same as a month's rent, which you pay to the landlord as security. The landlord can keep all or part of this money to cover repairs and cleaning. You should be given a receipt.

When you move in

Locate water and gas stopcocks and the electrical fuse box, in case of emergencies. Find the electricity and gas meters and take your own readings. Decide on home entertainment, such as freeview boxes, television rental, and cable or satellite television.

TV licence

If you watch TV and don't get a licence, you could be looking at a £1,000 fine, and your chances of getting caught are high. Call 0300 790 6131 for payments and rebates or use the website, www.tvlicensing.co.uk.

Communal items

It's easiest to put money for toilet rolls, bin bags, cleaning products, and shared food such as milk or margarine in a kitty. Or take turns buying them.

Bills

If you're struggling to pay any household bills, contact the supplier as soon as possible to let them know you are experiencing difficulty. There's often one person in a shared house who's late with the rent or forgets to pay their share of the bills, and if a flatmate has run off and left bills unpaid, contact the landlord and the supplier quickly. The landlord could give you money out of their deposit to cover the shortfall, or the company might let you off part of the bill.

Responsibilities of the landlord

Landlords must keep the following things in proper working order: exterior structure of the house, water, gas, electricity, sewerage, space heating and hot water. If there's anything wrong with your property, notify the landlord in writing as well as telephoning or emailing. Allow 48 hours for emergency works and one or two weeks for other works. If the landlord doesn't sort things out, you can speak to a Citizens Advice Bureau or the housing charity Shelter (see p. 227).

Harassment and illegal eviction

Your landlord (or their agent) is not allowed to:

- turn up unannounced and let themselves in, unless it's an emergency
- tamper with locks, electricity, gas or water
- interfere with possessions
- threaten violence or use force
- evict you without going through the correct legal process
- show sexual or racial discrimination.

If any of these happen, seek immediate help from your local council's tenancy relations officer or the charity Shelter.

Fire safety

If your house doesn't have smoke detectors, get some as soon as you can because smoke and fumes can kill quickly and silently. They only cost a few pounds and they're worth every penny.

Common causes of house fires are listed below.

- Candles: never leave them unattended.
- Cigarettes: don't smoke in bed.
- Kitchen fires: avoid using chip pans if you can. Put pan fires out by covering them with a damp wrung-out tea towel and turning the cooker off if possible. Leave the pan where it is, damp towel in place, until it has cooled.
- Heaters: don't cover them or knock them over while they're on, and don't hang clothes on them to dry unless they're standard radiators (no bar or flame).
- Electrical: report loose sockets to the landlord, and don't overload with plugs and extensions.

Keep fire exits free from rubbish or bicycles. Keep keys near to doors and windows to allow a speedy exit, but not in view of passing burglars. Go around the house to check the ashtrays and close the doors before you go to bed at night.

If you discover a fire:

- O raise the alarm by shouting loudly
- O get everyone out of the house without putting yourself at risk
- O shut doors behind you and call 999
- O if you're trapped upstairs, shut doors and stay low to avoid smoke, and throw bedding onto the ground to soften your landing; lower yourself out of the window
- O if you can't jump, keep your head out of the window to breathe fresh air, continue calling for help
- O if your clothes catch fire, roll on the floor to put the flames out.

Find out more about fire safety at www.firekills.direct.gov.uk.

Gas and carbon monoxide

Carbon monoxide is a silent killer, and causes around 30 unnecessary deaths every year. The gas can seep out of old or unserviced gas appliances, and be made worse by blocked chimneys and flues. Landlords are legally obliged to have every gas appliance checked yearly by a registered engineer, and should show you the safety certificate within one month. To check on any engineer, call the Gas Safe Register on 0800 408 5500 or visit www.gassaferegister.co.uk. Never block the ventilation that the appliances need, such as flues and air bricks. Although there might be no danger signs, make sure your appliances do not show any of the following: staining or discolouration, burning with a lazy orange or yellow flame, or a strange smell when in use. To be on the safe side, you can get a carbon monoxide detector.

Carbon monoxide poisoning is hard to detect, and the symptoms can resemble those of flu, food poisoning or depression. Be on the look out for headaches, dizziness, muscle weakness, tiredness, vomiting or nausea, diarrhoea, stomach pain, or chest pain. The symptoms can come on slowly, or be sudden. If you think there's a chance you have carbon monoxide poisoning, speak to your GP or go to the accident and emergency department at your local hospital.

Gas leaks are rare, but if you smell gas in your home:

- O immediately put out any lighted cigarettes
- O open doors and windows
- O turn off gas supply
- O don't switch anything electrical off or on, not even a light switch
- O get everyone out of the house and call Transco free on 0800 111 999.

You will get a free visit from an engineer. For more information look at www.nationalgrid.com/uk/Gas/Safety/Emergency.

Security at home

Be careful about who you let in, remember to lock up regularly, and follow a few security measures to reduce your chances of being burgled.

- If you're renting a place, pick one with sturdy doors, strong locks, and secure windows, preferably with a burglar alarm.
- Nag your landlord to provide decent locks on the front door and bedroom doors, a door chain and window locks.
- A visible burglar alarm can put off thieves.
- Try not to display valuables near your windows.
- If you're leaving your house unattended for a few days, ask friendly neighbours to keep an eye on the place and leave a contact phone number with them.
- Mark expensive items with an invisible UV pen. If they are stolen, there's a chance the police will be able to locate and return them to you.
- Don't leave spare door keys outside under the doormat or in a nearby plant pot. It's the first place a burglar will look.
- It's a really good idea get your belongings insured, just in case.

Your local police can give you more information about home safety measures.

Handling your money

If you don't know much about handling finances, now's a good time to start. Learn how to make and stick to a basic budget, and know how to use bank or credit cards without getting ripped off. Get into the habit of putting enough to one side for bills. If you don't know how to check and pay bills, ask a relative or your local Citizens Advice Bureau (see p. 222). If you mess up your budget don't give up completely, start again.

Basic budgeting skills

Once you know your basic living costs, start making a budget. Work it out on a monthly or weekly basis. Write your budgets down and try your hardest to stick to them. Keep track of everything you spend, and review regularly.

One way to cope with a tight budget is by working in cash for weekly spending. Put the cash card away somewhere safe. This leaves money for groceries, toiletries, the laundrette, travel, going out and so on. Once it's gone, don't go back to the bank for more. For more help with your budgeting skills, try reading *Money for Life* by Alvin Hall (Coronet, £5.99), or visit www.lovemoney.com and www.moneysavingexpert.com.

Money saving tips

General tips.

- Claim all benefits for prescription charges, dental care, and so on.
- Some bills are cheaper if you pay by direct debit.
- Cut transport costs by cycling, or using discount cards.

Utilities bills.

- Shop around for gas, electricity, telephone, and internet connection deals. Try online price comparison services.
- If you are sent an estimate for a bill, read the meter yourself.
- Don't leave televisions on standby.
- Switch your thermostat down half a degree.
- Don't boil a kettle full of water for one cup of tea.

Mobile phone bills.

- Although the cost per unit is higher, a pay-as-you-go mobile is the easiest way to keep your total bill manageable.
- If you're disciplined, a good line rental deal might be cheaper. Shop around.
- If your mate is a chatterbox, send them a text message instead.
- Use free email, messenger and Skype software.

Food bills.

- Buy in bulk with friends or flatmates.
- Go to fruit and vegetable markets just before they close.
- Buy from bargain supermarkets (Aldi, Lidl or Netto), or stick to bargain ranges.
- Make meals at home based on cheap filling foods such as pasta, rice, potatoes, beans or bread.
- Buy seasonal local fruit and vegetables, and fish or meat.
- Plan weekly recipes and food shopping, and write down a shopping list.
- Don't buy too many takeaways or ready meals.

Credit cards

Cards are the most expensive way to borrow. Anyone who uses them as a long-term way to borrow lots of money can carry crippling debt for years. They're useful sometimes, for instance when you are travelling, but read the small print. Store cards are another type of credit card, and they often charge very high levels of interest.

Card fraud

Keep a note of card numbers and emergency card theft hotlines at home in case your wallet or bag gets stolen. Don't let cards out of your sight during transactions in shops or restaurants in case they get 'skimmed' (someone runs your card through a tiny reader, then the number is used to obtain goods without your knowledge). Report stolen cards to the issuer immediately. When shopping on the internet, use well-known websites with secure services, and never put your full card number into an email. Check statements every month for unexpected purchases.

Debt problems

It's easy to get into debt if you aren't used to handling your finances, but try to sort things out before they get worse. If you're about to go over your agreed overdraft limit, phone the bank immediately to avoid the fees and interest charges. There are several signs that suggest you're building up an unmanageable debt.

- You're too scared to work out how much you owe in total.
- You avoid opening your bank statements and bills, throw them away, or hide them.
- You can barely cover each minimum monthly credit card repayment.
- You let unauthorised overdrafts build up, because you can't talk to the bank.
- You're taking out loans or other credit to pay off other debts.
- You get angry letters from creditors, threats of eviction or visits from bailiffs.

How to sort bad debts out

- If your debts are out of control, the first thing to do is admit there's a serious problem.
- Work out exactly how much you do owe, and to whom. List everything: overdraft, loans, credit cards, money owed to friends and family, hire-purchase agreements, and so on. Then prioritise these debts while you get a handle on your spending.
- Your main aim is to keep a roof over your head, and to avoid getting your utilities cut off – make sure your rent and bills are covered first.
- Make a strict budget for your everyday outgoings, and stick to it, even if that means unpleasant cutbacks.
- Target anything that's being charged at higher rates of interest, such as credit cards, and sort that out as a priority. Wherever possible, switch the balance onto cards with lower Annual Percentage Rates (APRs] so you're paying as little interest as possible. Then tackle the remaining debts with high interest charges.
- Make a debt repayment plan, with help from one of the non-profit organisations listed on page 227, including what you're able to pay everyone each month.

If you've missed any payments, write to the companies involved, and explain your financial situation. Offer to make reduced payments and pay the debt off over a longer period of time. Most companies will agree (it costs more to take legal action against you or send in bailiffs). If anyone is threatening you with court proceedings, or has already started them, you urgently need advice from an organisation such as a Citizens Advice Bureau (see p. 222), or the National Debtline (call 0808 808 4000). Harassment from your creditors, such as making nuisance visits and phone calls, or using threatening and abusive language is illegal.

Although it's tempting, avoid commercial companies that offer to consolidate debts. There are several free advice services that can help you to manage your debts much more effectively, so use them instead. Some people choose to be declared bankrupt to avoid their creditors, but think very carefully about this option. Assets might still be taken to pay off your debts, you'll have to close your bank or building society account, and it can damage your credit rating for years.

Chapter 7
Further information

This chapter will help you to track down the right advice and information from a range of useful services and contacts.

Careers advice and work rights

Connexions Direct

A support service for young people aged 13–19 in England, Connexions can offer advice on anything from choosing the right courses and careers to drug abuse and homelessness. The service is managed locally and if you contact your local partnership then you can make arrangements to speak in confidence with a Connexions personal adviser.

Freephone: 080 800 13219
www.connexions-direct.com

Jobs4U Database

A large careers database maintained by the Connexions service, containing job profiles, entry requirements, job market information, careers prospects and many useful contacts.

www.connexions-direct.com/Jobs4u

Regional careers services

Careers Service Northern Ireland

Tel: 028 9044 1781
www.careersserviceni.com

Careers Scotland

Freephone: 0845 8 502 502
www.careers-scotland.org

Careers Wales

Tel: 0800 100 900
www.careerswales.com

Learndirect

Speak to a trained adviser on any aspect of your career, training or education options. Learndirect is mainly aimed at adults but is open to anyone regardless of age.

Tel: 08000 150 450
www.learndirect.co.uk

Your local 14–19 Prospectus

This website lists all the training, education and employment options open to you in the area that you live in.

http://yp.direct.gov.uk/14-19prospectus/

Citizens Advice Bureau

This organisation offers a wide range of consumer, money and work advice to people around the UK via local offices, helplines and websites. Its Advice Guide website also contains a very helpful section for young workers.

www.citizensadvice.org.uk

www.adviceguide.org.uk/index/your_money/employment/young_people_and_employment.htm

Input Youth

Job guides, careers advice, news and site links, providing information and help on a variety of youth-related subjects.

www.inputyouth.co.uk

Other useful general advice websites for young workers are:

- ○ www.need2know.co.uk
- ○ www.nya.org.uk/youthinformation-com
- ○ www.readyforwork.org
- ○ www.my-work-experience.com.

Young Workers (workplace safety from RoSPA)

This website is aimed at young people who are taking part in work experience programmes or who are starting work for the first time. Here you will find all kinds of information about health and safety in the workplace, including your responsibilities at work, facts and figures about risks and injuries at work, and guidance and checklists to help you through your first few days at work.

www.youngworker.co.uk

Pay and Work Rights Helpline

This confidential helpline provides help and advice on government-enforced employment rights. It provides information on national minimum wage rights, agricultural minimum wage rights, and the right not to have to work more than 48 hours a week against your will. You can also phone the helpline for information about the employment rights that apply if you are paid by an employment agency or gangmaster.

Tel: 0800 917 2368
Text phone: 0800 121 4042
http://payandworkrightscampaign.direct.gov.uk

Acas Helpline

The Acas Helpline is the place to go for both employers and employees who are involved in an employment dispute or are seeking information on employment rights and rules. The helpline provides clear, confidential, independent and impartial advice to assist you in resolving issues in the workplace.

Tel: 08457 47 47 47 Monday–Friday, 8.00a.m. to 8.00p.m., or Saturday, 9.00a.m. to 1.00p.m.
www.acas.gov.uk

Jobcentre Plus

Jobcentre Plus provides a wide range of information and services, such as benefits, loans and grants and help with finding a job.

- If you need to make a claim for benefit call 0800 055 6688. If you find it hard to speak or hear clearly a textphone is available on 0800 023 4888. Lines are open from 8.00a.m. to 6.00p.m., Monday to Friday.
- You can also search for a job on telephone. To use the Jobcentre Plus phone service call 0845 6060 234. If you find it hard to speak or hear clearly a textphone is available on 0845 6055 255. Lines are open between 8.00a.m. and 6.00p.m. from Monday to Friday, and between 9.00a.m. and 1.00p.m. on Saturdays.

Discrimination and Disputes at Work

This website gives the government's advice on discrimination at work and resolving workplace disputes.

www.direct.gov.uk/en/Employment/ResolvingWorkplaceDisputes/DiscriminationAt Work/index.htm

WorkSMART

This website has information on apprentice rights and joining a union.
www.worksmart.org.uk

Skill

Skill is the national bureau for students and trainees with disabilities and over the age of 16 who are interested in education, training or employment.

Helpline: 0800 328 5050, open Tuesdays 11.30a.m. to 1.30p.m. and Thursdays 1.30p.m. to 3.30p.m.

To contact Skill Scotland direct: call 0131 475 2348.

Free Textphone for hearing or speech-impaired callers: 18001 0800 328 5050

Email: info@skill.org.uk

SMS text: If you are aged between 16–24 text to 07786 208 028

Fax: 020 7450 0650

Post: Skill, Unit 3, Floor 3, Radisson Court, 219 Long Lane, London SE1 4PR

www.skill.org.uk

Sector skills councils

Get the best advice on the skills you need to learn to get on in your chosen career.

Asset Skills

This website has advice on facilities management, housing, property, planning, cleaning and parking.

www.assetskills.org

Cogent

Visit this website to learn about chemicals and pharmaceuticals, oil and gas, nuclear, petroleum and polymer industries.

www.cogent-ssc.com

ConstructionSkills

This website has information about every part of the construction industry.

www.cskills.org

Creative and Cultural Skills

Access the websites listed below for more information about working in advertising, crafts, cultural heritage, design, music, performing, literary and visual arts.

www.ccskills.org.uk
www.creative-choices.co.uk

e-skills uk

This is the website for checking out business and information technology.

www.e-skills.com

Energy & Utility Skills
This website will tell you about electricity, gas, waste management and water industries.

www.euskills.co.uk

Financial Services Skills Council
Visit this website for advice on financial services, accountancy and finance.

www.fssc.org.uk

GoSkills
Get information on passenger transport industries on this website.

www.goskills.org

Government Skills
For information about central government, all civil service departments and agencies, unaffiliated non-departmental government bodies and the armed forces, visit this website.

www.government-skills.gov.uk

IMI
This website will give you advice on work in the automotive retail industries.

www.motor.org.uk

Improve Ltd
This website has information about food and drink manufacturing and processing.

www.improveltd.co.uk

Lantra
For information on land management and production, animal health and welfare and environmental industries, visit this website.

www.lantra.co.uk

Lifelong Learning UK
This website has information on community learning and development, further education, higher education, libraries, archives and information services and work-based learning.

www.lluk.org

People 1st
Find out more about contract food service providers, events, gambling, holiday parks, hospitality services, hostels, hotels, membership clubs, pubs, bars and nightclubs, restaurants,

self-catering accommodation, tourist services, travel services and visitor attractions at this website.

www.people1st.co.uk

Proskills

Visit this website to learn about building products, coatings, extractive and mineral processing, furniture, furnishings and interiors, glass and glazing, glazed ceramics, paper and printing industries.

www.proskills.co.uk

Semta

This website will tell you about science, engineering and manufacturing technologies: aerospace, automotive, bioscience, electrical, electronics, maintenance, marine, mathematics, mechanical, metals and engineered metal products industries.

www.semta.org.uk

Skills for Care and Development

This website will tell you about social care, children, early years and young people's workforce in the UK.

www.skillsforcareanddevelopment.org.uk

Skills for Health

Use this website to check out work opportunities in health and healthcare.

www.skillsforhealth.org.uk

Skills for Justice

This website has information on the justice sector.

www.skillsforjustice.com

Skills for Logistics

This website will tell you about working in the freight logistics industries.

www.skillsforlogistics.org

SkillsActive

Get information on working in the active leisure and learning industry from this website: sport and fitness, outdoors and adventure, playwork, camping and caravanning.

www.skillsactive.com

Skillset

Visit this website to learn about creative media (advertising, animation, computer games, facilities, film, interactive media, photo imaging, publishing, radio and television) and the fashion and textiles industry (design, manufacturing and servicing of clothing, footwear and textile fabrics).

www.skillset.org

Skillsmart Retail

Get information on the retail sector from this website.

www.skillsmartretail.com

SummitSkills

This website will tell you about building services engineering: electro-technical, heating, ventilating, air conditioning, refrigeration and plumbing industries.

www.summitskills.org.uk

Help with money management

What About Money?

What About Money is the website to get free impartial information on money and financial matters for all 16–24 year olds, including students and graduates.

The Moneymadeclear service gives you impartial information and guidance about your money to help you work out what's right for you. It won't try to sell you anything and won't recommend specific products or providers. Moneymadeclear is run by the Consumer Financial Education Body (CFEB).

www.whataboutmoney.info

Help with housing problems

Shelter

Shelter is a housing charity that runs a housing helpline, has a network of housing aid centres, and works with local citizens advice bureaus. If you are having any housing problems, from contracts, to difficult landlords, to being made homeless, you can go to Shelter for advice.

For urgent housing advice call 0808 800 4444, 8a.m. to 8p.m. Monday to Friday, and 8a.m. to 5p.m. on Saturday and Sunday.

www.shelter.org.uk

Glossary

Agricultural Minimum Wage – The minimum rate of payment for any type of agricultural work, which is set by the Agricultural Wages Board

Apprenticeship – Working for skilled and qualified people to learn a trade or profession, usually for a set length of time

Bonus system – An offer of extra money on top of a person's wages that will be paid if targets are met

Client – The customer, or user of a service

Commission – A percentage of the money made during a sale that is given to a salesperson, on top of their regular wages

Contractor – A person or business that supplies material or labour to another business

CV – Short for curriculum vitae. A written record of a person's experience, skills and qualifications to show to employers

Employee – Someone who has been hired to work for an organisation

Enterprise skills – The skills needed to set up or run a successful business, such as market research, teamwork, problem-solving and fundraising

Freelancer – A self-employed person who works on projects for clients

Gangmaster – The supervisor or employer of a group of workers, most commonly workers who are doing temporary work on farms

Human resources – A department in an organisation that is responsible for hiring staff, and looking after their welfare

Labour market – An area in which workers compete for jobs and employers compete for workers

Networking – Meeting and keeping in touch with business contacts to build relationships and swap information

NHS – National Health Service

Overtime – Working more than the hours agreed in a contract, sometimes for extra payment

Payslip – A written record of payment and tax that comes with wages

Portfolio – A collection of your best work to show to clients or employers

Promotion – Moving up to a more senior or skilled job, often with a pay increase

Recruitment – Hiring people for work

Recruitment agency – A business that finds vacancies for jobseekers with a range of employers, and is paid by employers for placing new staff with them

Redundancy – Losing a job because the employer no longer needs that work to be done (often so that the business can operate more efficiently)

References – Written or verbal comments given to an employer (often from a past employer, teacher or other responsible person) that show you are suitable for a job and are a reliable worker

Self-employed – Someone who runs their own business

Shift work – A set pattern of working hours that might include working early mornings or late nights

Staff – People who are employed by an organisation

State Pension – A regular payment that people can claim from the government when they reach retirement age, which varies according to the amount of tax they have paid during their working life

Technician – A person who is skilled at mechanical, industrial, laboratory or artistic work

Transferable skills – Skills developed through training and experience that are useful if a person moves to another type of job, including communication skills, IT skills and critical thinking

Vacancy – A job opportunity

Vocational training – Work-based training that is mainly practical

Wages – Regular payments for work

Wholesale trade – Where businesses buy stock from other businesses, usually in large quantities and at lower cost than standard public retail prices